DATE DUE

Managing Success

MANAGING SUCCESS

High-Echelon Careers and Motherhood

Aasta S. Lubin

COLUMBIA UNIVERSITY PRESS
New York 1987

Library of Congress Cataloging-in-Publication Data

Lubin, Aasta S.
Managing success.

Bibliography: p.
Includes index.
1. Working mothers—United States—Biography.
2. Mothers—Employment—United States. I. Title.
HQ759.48.L83   1987   306.8'7   86-19274
ISBN 0-231-06142-0

Columbia University Press
New York   Guildford, Surrey
Copyright © 1987 Columbia University Press
All rights reserved
Printed in the United States of America

Book design by Ken Venezio

For My Daughter Karin Ann

Contents

Acknowledgments

I wish to thank Professor Herve Varenne of the Department of Family and Community Education, Teachers College, Columbia University for his guidance throughout the project, Barbara Glaser for her patient help in editing the original manuscript, and Professor Emeritus Mackie L. Jarrell for her invaluable suggestions and help in revising the manuscript of the book. To all the women who participated and shared their time and lives with me, my special gratitude.

Managing Success

Introduction

Successful career women who are also wives and mothers belong to a small minority of American working women. Yet they have caught the attention of the media to an extraordinary extent and are a frequent topic of discussion, often of a contradictory nature. Tagged with such labels as "Superwoman," "The Total Woman," and "The Woman Who Has It All," women of this kind are held in awe, envied, admired, and criticized. They live on the cutting edge of change.

Women in the success subculture described in this book are a microcosm of a societal drama taking place in today's America. Their lives are very different from what stereotypes and myths tell us is proper for women. Their major advantage is their sizable income, which to some degree frees them to experiment, to wrest themselves loose from old expectations and to create new ones for themselves as career women, wives, mothers, and social beings. They do not have role models—nor do their husbands. The families share in the experimentation.

The drama is created by forces—economic, political, psychological, historical, cultural, and institutional—that are involved in a complex power play, intricately affecting and reshaping one another. Research by women on women is proliferating, on women's psychology and role in the family and in the society. The psychology of women is being redefined on the basis of perceptions and experiences of women themselves. Studies are emerging on the effect changes have on children, husbands, and fathers. Men are experimenting with new roles in the family. A more nurturing role with their children and more sharing in household tasks is now a familiar pattern.

The women discussed here are all of the baby-boom generation, born after World War II. Along with other women, they are reaping the benefits of the changes taking place as a consequence of Title VII of the Civil Rights Act and of the women's movement. They took advantage of the openings beginning to occur in the business and the professional world. Actually, many of the women I met during my research started out in traditional women's professions, but switched careers when opportunities opened up in the so-called male professions. As a whole the number of women entering graduate schools and joining the traditional male professions in the last couple of decades has grown immensely. For example, the Columbia University Graduate School of Business (1982) reports a jump in the number of female MBA graduates from 5 in 1960 to 245 in 1981. Nonetheless, the success stories are still few. Women have always been channeled into the lower-rung jobs, as is clearly demonstrated by Epstein (1970) in *Woman's Place* and by Kanter (1977) in *Men and Women of the Corporation*. If women do manage to break out of this pattern in greater numbers, accommodations will have to be made for them, and competition will become even fiercer than it is today.

Kanter thinks that the structure of the complex organizations routinely disadvantages some people, both men and women. The disadvantages in turn generate defeatist behavior. On the other hand, the prospect of increasing opportunities and power offered a class of advantaged persons in the organization does not necessarily have "desirable consequences, for those people may become more involved with the politics of climbing than the human side of the organization or the personal side of life" (Kanter 1982:247). The women I came to know well through my research appear to have succeeded in avoiding both pitfalls Kanter mentions.

Through pressure, with the help of the law and affirmative action, women have now managed to reach middle-management levels in much greater numbers than before, but they seem to be held at bay there in the hierarchical structure. The upper tiers are still occupied by men only. A few women, like the ones in this study, who have gone beyond middle management are in a kind of gray zone between middle and top management, but at least they are close to the top. Since women are not included in the "old boys' club," women in the success subculture are establishing their own network by forming strong professional women's organizations. Through these they are gaining power and thereby leverage for upward mobility. Many have no doubt that they will reach senior executive positions. Others are finding routes to the top by starting their own businesses. It is clear that neither women nor men can succeed without support systems.

Some observers, including sociologists Hunt and Hunt (1982a), argue that in dual-career families "internal and external resources" will be in short supply. They think that developing one career is a "two-person" job that needs a wife not working outside the home. They further maintain that with the addition of many women to the labor market, competition will be so stiff that the "two-person career" family will win out because, so the Hunts believe, it will have more resources (1982a:181–91). If the steady increase of married women in the labor force continues—and there are no indications that it will not—their view will be outdated in a few years despite the apparent resistance in public opinion. My study contradicts the "two-person career" view for another reason, which is, in fact, one of my most interesting realizations: it requires many more than two people to make one successful career. Here is the explanation of why almost all the successful women described in the book have successful husbands too. There is always what I have come to call a "sustaining crowd" around a successful career.

My own point of view is similar to that expressed by Epstein (1983) in an article in *Working Woman* about women comparable with those in this study. She writes:

It may well be time to take stock of the cost of success, but it is also time to separate truth from fiction about what the costs are, and to whom, and what can be done about them. Must carrying a variety of roles inevitably produce a frenzied and frazzled life? Is this peculiarly a woman's problem? (Epstein 1983:100)

This study will try to answer these questions, take stock of the cost of success, and separate fact from fiction about a group of successful women. I see these women as general managers of particular social systems consisting of career, marriage, children, and social life. The functioning of the women and that of the various members of their "sustaining crowd" are the issues described in this book.

As general managers, the women must use themselves and their support systems effectively, decide on priorities. We shall see the strategies they employ in doing so, as well as what can go wrong. The women in my study live in New York City, a place with vast resources for working women who can afford to use them. Private schools, live-in or live-out housekeepers, babysitters, cleaning people, caterers, restaurants, stores, hairdressers, you name it are available to some extent both day and night. These resources are an integral part of the support systems that sustain successful career women and their families.

Obviously, managerial skills are needed to handle the necessary support systems. Many such skills can be learned. The job of the general manager is unquestionably demanding. Certain personality attributes and attitudes seem to be prerequisite to success for men and women alike, as is suggested by the professional literature. Women, however, are still at a disadvantage in today's society in comparison to men. They are discriminated against and they carry a "psychological baggage" different from that of men. Men have society's sanction in regard to work, while women working outside the home often do not.

The five busy women who have permitted me to intrude upon their lives and families for the purposes of my research are all successful professional career women and live in New York City. They have reached high-echelon positions in their organizations and earn well in excess of $50,000 a year. All are married and have young children of preschool or early school age. New York City is a major financial center and was therefore likely to provide a good, diversified pool of women from which to choose. It was a natural and convenient criterion. However, women belonging to the success subculture can be found all across the country.

The plan of my research was to learn from the women themselves how they handle their many roles, how they see themselves, how they run their days, how they are viewed by the people around them, how many people are necessary to their success. The major part of the study is a detailed description of the women's lives as told to and observed by me in their homes and offices, in meetings and in restaurants.

This is an ethnographic study. "Ethnography," writes Spradley (1979:3), "is the work of describing a culture. . . . The goal of ethnography, as Malinowski put it, is 'to grasp the native's point of view, his relation to life, to realize *his* vision of *his* world. . . .' (1922:25). Rather than *studying people*, ethnography means *learning from people*." It is essential to learn people's language. Studying a subculture of people who "*appear* to use a language identical to that spoken by the ethnographer" requires caution because "semantic differences exist and they have profound influence on ethnographic research" (Spradley 1979:18). Before I could learn how my informants function, as the reader will see in chapter 2, I had to learn "the language of success." One must understand the meaning of people's concept of things in their own terms, not in terms based on one's own value system, which would give a distorted picture. Therefore, this book attempts to avoid value judgments. The women have carved out the ways they want to live. It is immaterial whether one thinks the way is good, bad, or indifferent.

When an anthropologist goes to study in a different culture, she learns the language and observes the daily routine and customs. She gets to know people, some better than others. In sum, she learns much of the information firsthand. The goal is to describe how people see their world, and to catalogue the customs they accept and expect as requisites to belonging. The people are *informants* as distinct from subjects being studied.

This book, then, is not a survey designed to sample characteristics of people of a certain type. What we learn about the characteristics of the informants is incidental. Neither is it quantitative; it doesn't tell us how many women in the success subculture are married or have one or two children, how many spend more time at work than with their families, and so on. An ethnographic study is needed to show us what questions to ask—what regularities appear, what variables suggest themselves. Many facets of the success subculture might be interesting to pursue in other research.

For example, there may be a difference in the lifestyles of successful women who are ten to fifteen years older than the women in this study, all of whom came into the work force at approximately the same time (late 1960s to early 1970s) and are all in their thirties and of white middle-class background. Possibly there are differences between them and the new generation of women entering the world of work now. Minority women, owing to the differences in cultural backgrounds and the added dimension of minority discrimination, probably have diverse experiences, lives, and support systems from those of the women in this study.

When I began my study, I decided that the best way to learn about the world of the successful career woman and mother was through interviewing and participant observation. First I conducted a pilot study, interviewing ten women in depth. I covered the same aspects with everyone, leaving the interviews as open-ended as possible. The aspects covered were family background, education, job history, how they saw themselves having reached their present level, marriages, pregnancies, how these affected their careers, their daily life and work, sex discrimination they encountered, goals, and mentors. The interviews lasted from 1½ to 2 hours and were generally followed up with a second interview of approximately the same length. The women were chosen haphazardly although selected to fit specific criteria. The main source of contact came through a Working Mothers' group that had spun off from an organization of professionals to which the women belong. The chairperson of the group facilitated my entry into it. I approached some women by telephone and some at the Working Mothers' monthly luncheons. No one refused.

On the basis of these interviews, I decided rather arbitrarily on criteria for the successful career woman in the study proper. She had to have a high-echelon job. (She was often the first woman in her position.) Her income should be over $50,000. (My informants earn a good deal more than this amount.) She also had to be a mother of young children and to live in New York City.

I wanted to get to know five women well and to talk with people they interact with, such as husbands, children, housekeepers, friends, relatives, secretaries, and bosses. It was left to the discretion of the informants to whom I would have access. The five women were equally haphazardly chosen. One I happened to meet socially, two were in the pilot study and fitted the criteria, one was a panel member at a meeting I attended, and, finally, one I sat next to at a Working Mothers' luncheon. They all expressed their willingness to participate in the study. Four of my informants are from the financial business community and one is from an international organization. As it happened all are married. They range in age from 32 to 37 years old. They are white from middle- and upper-middle-class backgrounds, and entered the work world with at least a college education. All now have graduate degrees; three of them obtained an MBA degree while working. Of their children the oldest is 5 years of age. None have more than two children; two have stepchildren not living with them. I will present a portrait of each in chapter 1.

I followed two of them around from early morning until almost bedtime, keeping a log of what one day was like for them (see the appendix). All were interviewed in depth, and all were visited in their homes with their husbands and children present. I saw their offices, interviewed two secretaries and two housekeepers, and talked to all their husbands and saw all their children, except stepchildren. I also talked with the parents of one informant and a friend of another and met one boss.

One woman, Jean, from the pilot study, is quoted extensively throughout the book. She fits the criteria, but is not included in the study proper because she is viewed as exceptional—"a superwoman"— by her female colleagues. She is therefore not in the mainstream of the success subculture but is interesting as a comparison with the others. Her activity and energy are described particularly in the chapter on social activities. A few other women were described similarly by their colleagues in the success subculture but I never met them personally.

I attended twelve Working Mothers' luncheons and five meetings of the professional organization's Career Roundtable discussions on Life/Work/Style. The attendance at the luncheons ranged from 8 to 31 participants, mostly working mothers. Twice one father was present. Some women who were contemplating having children attended. Nonmembers were welcome. At the roundtable discussions there were from 23 to 40 in attendance. Attending gave me a unique opportunity to see most of my informants as well as other career women interact with each other and to hear them present their lives, work, and styles, both as panel members and in fielding questions from the audience. At luncheons I was able to observe the women in informal interaction, learning a great deal about their thinking. They generally had nonpaid speakers at these luncheons who talked about topics such as "The Transition from Being Child-Focused to Being Family-Focused," "The Decision to Have a Second Child," "Feeling Good—Building Self-Esteem in Children," "Independence: Yours or Theirs" (a parent discussion with a consultant), "Child Development: The Early Years," "Stress in the Dual-Career Marriage," "Stress and Motherhood," and "Discipline." They asked interested questions and offered information on how they handled personal situations. They were quite candid about their experiences and concerns.

Theirs is a lifestyle of juggling roles, of compromises and trade-offs. According to my informants, it all is compensated for by their career achievements, their husbands, their children, and their financial comforts. Nevertheless, a majority at one luncheon agreed—by vote—that if it was at all feasible and would not affect their careers, they might work one or two days less on their jobs, partly in order to spend more time with their children but primarily to have some time to themselves. They all emphatically rejected the idea of staying at home full time.

As a participant observer, I took the tape recorder with me everywhere. Everything was taped—in offices, homes, restaurants, and meetings, except for a few of the Working

Mothers' luncheons. Here, in the beginning, I was concerned that the taping might be resented. As I became a familiar figure and people knew what I was doing, I felt comfortable asking if I could tape. The answer, by then, I knew: "Of course, no problem." Quotations in this book are verbatim, transcribed from tapes. All names have been changed.

In analyzing the data I collected, I look at the material quality of the women's lives. This includes the essential things that must be done by the woman herself, the things she can delegate, and the things she chooses to do herself. These activities are separated into six categories to be dealt with in individual chapters. Each category is analyzed in terms of systems theory, that is, broken into its components and tasks. I do this to show the interdependence of the components and the balance needed for the social system to run smoothly. If one link is weak, it needs reinforcement or replacement; otherwise stress will occur. For example, if a housekeeper is sick, temporary substitutes or other arrangements will have to be found. Until the housekeeper returns or a new one is found, a certain amount of discomfort is felt by everyone in the household.

The woman and all the components of her life are viewed as an organization—a kind of company with component departments—where she emerges as the general manager. There is no one best way of organizing; that depends entirely on each idiosyncratic family, its values, and the resources available to it. The husband may be the part-time administrative assistant, the comptroller, the chairman of the board, or a combination of these, depending on the individual system. This kind of analysis enables me to demystify the complexity of the women's lives and sort out reality from fiction. It makes it understandable how the system works, and possibly points to reasons why it may not work for some. These women all have certain abilities and personality characteristics necessary to be a general manager.

To find the women's pattern of management, questions that need to be answered are the following: (1) Is it pragmatically possible for a successful woman to manage her social system and run it smoothly without wearing herself out, whether she works 45 hours or 75 hours weekly? (2) If so, how can this be done? (3) What part is played by the demands of her career and what part by commitment to the career and/or the family. (4) What happens if there is a poor fit between the career and the family? (5) Using a system analysis in such a situation, what changes can or need be made? (6) Where do the husband and child fit into the system? (7) What support systems are involved in running the woman's social system? (8) How does it compare with a man's social system?

The book details the numerous factors and complexities that are involved in maintaining the social and financial success of the women in the success subculture. This information is generalizable and may be helpful to women who are in this subculture or want to enter it.

1

Portraits of the
Main Informants

To set the stage, I would like to introduce the five women who allowed me to step into their lives and who shared so much of themselves with me. Since this is not a psychological study, the only background information I needed was the essentials about their family constellation and their parents' socioeconomic and cultural background. Whatever else I learned depended a great deal on the individual woman, the timing, and the circumstances under which they spoke with me. Information on education, career development, and related issues was also informally obtained.

Two of the women, Anna and Karin, were born and grew up in Europe. Anna is married to an American and has worked in the success subculture for many years. Karin is less acculturated, I think, than Anna. She went to college and graduate school in America and has lived here a few years since, but her husband is not American. Nevertheless, both women accept the values and meet the standards of the success subculture.

Here, then, are their stories.

Anna, Director of Planning, publishing firm. Age, 34. Husband, Robert, 38 years old, Supervisor, Educational System. Child, Michael, 3½ years old.

Anna was born in Europe, on a farm, and lived there until she was 5 years old. Her parents had started a small country store. When it became successful, they moved the family to a nearby small town where they built the store into a thriving shopping center. The family lived over the store. Her father was the planner, and her mother handled the accounting side of the business. Her oldest brother now runs the family business. Anna is the second oldest of 6 children, 3 brothers and 3 sisters. Her oldest brother is 37 years old, and the youngest sibling, a brother, is 23. All her siblings are well educated. One sister and her husband, with their baby, are currently students in upstate New York. Anna comments on how easy she thought it must be to have children, because her mother would just retreat upstairs to deliver a child and reappear at work almost right away.

Anna, in fact, often expresses incredulity at the interest in the career woman and mother. "It seems so ordinary, so boring," she repeats. Once she commented, "You know what women on farms do. They get up at 4–5 A.M. and go out to milk the cows, taking the little kids with them because they can't be left alone at the house. Then back to feed everybody breakfast, and it continues like that all day. What we do is nothing. My mother with six kids was looked at as lucky because she had household help, but she had *six* kids. It's all relative, you know."

Anna, a pretty woman with beautiful coloring, wears no makeup. She has a quiet charm and a forthright manner.

After graduating from business college in her country, majoring in marketing and business law, she came to the United States on an exchange program for a year. She met her husband on a two-months' stay in New York City on her way home. After a whirlwind courtship, including a visit by Robert with Anna and her family in the summer, he proposed via long-distance telephone on his return to the United States. She left her family behind, returned to New York, and married Robert thirteen years ago.

Anna started out in low-rung jobs in accounting. "Really the pits," she remarks. Had she gone into business in her own country, she would have started at a professional level. Accounting is not her cup of tea. After a few moves in unhappy jobs, she came to her present firm, where she has been for ten years. She moved to different areas within the company, gathering experience and working for many people who have since moved into important jobs. She thinks their knowledge of her good work helped her move steadily up the ladder. She obtained her MBA at night while working.

Her career was interrupted for more than a year by a miscarriage and a subsequent pregnancy, although she worked in between. She returned to a position equivalent to the one she had when she left. She now is in an important staff position with the opportunity to move on, including moving into a line position if she chooses. She and her husband work in entirely unrelated fields. She thinks it is difficult for Robert to comprehend the workings of the corporate world, being in a civil service bureaucracy himself. Anna says that she finds it hard to visualize what his job is like, although they do discuss work at home. He has a graduate degree in his field. They own a co-op and a newly acquired country house and have a live-out nursemaid.

Karin, Deputy Director. Age, 37. Husband, Andre, in his 30s, graduate student. Children, Lise, 2 years old, and Marcel, 4 months old.

Karin in contrast was born to what she terms a "patrician" family in Europe. Her father, now retired, was in the diplomatic service. Consequently she has lived in many countries and speaks several languages (seven, I believe). Karin's brother is 10 years older and is in the diplomatic service. Her sister (deceased) was 7 years older.

Her mother never did any cooking or housework; there were always servants. Her father was stationed in their native country until Karin was 7 years old. She seldom had a nanny and then only when the diplomatic etiquette of the country in which they were posted required that they have one. Her mother always took care of her. The nanny, according to Karin, was just another friendly person around.

Her mother is rather an unusual person. Karin talks admiringly of her. She did many out-of-the-ordinary things as a young woman, especially for those days. For example, she ran a poultry farm by herself in the south of France (not her native country). She learned to mountain climb when she was 49 years old, still climbs, and loves to take long hikes in the mountains. She is now in her seventies. She suffers from asthma.

Karin's parents, who live in the Alps, spell each other in staying with her here to help her out while Andre is away getting his graduate degree. Her mother cooks for Karen when she visits. Her father laughingly comments, "Yes, she cooked, but you didn't have to taste it." He is a gourmet cook who, in addition to cooking for the family every day when it is his turn to visit, also cooks for Karin's parties. He had made dinner for twenty people the night before I met him. He is a jovial, urbane man who speaks in glowing terms about his daughter's many proficiencies, both academic and athletic. He told stories of how even as a small child Karin knew how to handle people and situations.

Karin is a tall, attractive, energetic woman who generally walks and acts at a brisk pace. She wears no makeup; she is both straightforward and thoughtful in her manner. There is an eagerness about her. She continually switches languages while talking to various people. She is politically and socially aware.

She has a master's degree in her specialty from Harvard University. She met her husband while working in an underdeveloped country where he also had a job. Not many thought a young woman could succeed in her high-level position in a culture that places women extremely low on the totem pole. She *did* succeed and as a result was offered an important job opportunity in the Far East. They married and he went with her, losing about two years from his career. She was the first from her organization to arrive and built it up from scratch. Karin is now in New York City, while her husband is finishing his graduate work in another city, commuting here every other weekend for three to four days. They have a sublet apartment but need to find another by the end of the summer. She has a live-out housekeeper.

Karin is the youngest among both men and women at her level. She had accelerated promotions. She is very conscious of people's envy of her job and is particularly careful not to let her being a mother interfere with her job responsibilities.

The day I followed her around, she had been up nursing the baby twice during the night. He is now being weaned to the bottle. She went in one stretch from about 7 A.M., with a brief lunch, until 10–11 P.M. (See the appendix).

Sandy, First Vice President. Age, 35. Husband, Richard, in early 40s, Executive Vice President. Children, Elizabeth, 5 years old; second child due this summer; stepchildren, two adolescent girls, not living with them.

Sandy is of Irish-Catholic background. Her maternal grandmother, she tells me, came to America as a chattel maid. Her father put himself through college and became a manager in an insurance firm on Wall Street. Her mother finished high school and worked as a secretary until Sandy, the oldest child, was born. Sandy has 5 siblings, 3 brothers and 2 sisters. The youngest, a sister, is 12 years younger than Sandy.

The family moved to an affluent suburb when Sandy was 4 years old. Although they didn't want for anything, money was clearly somewhat scarce for them in comparison with their neighbors. Sandy went to parochial schools. In high school she was tutored in mathematics by the principal because the school's program did not fit Sandy's needs. She views the principal (a woman) as a significant role model. They often discussed issues together. Sandy, to her surprise, was elected class president in her freshman year. It was the first time she realized she had leadership qualities. She talks with enthusiasm about her father's habit of involving the children in stimulating table discussions about his work.

Sandy pokes fun at her parochial, rather cloistered background. The family spent two years in California when her father was transferred. That was the first time she was exposed to non-Catholics. "I didn't know there was anything else." She went to a state university in New York. The setting was highly competitive, her first experience with serious competition. She majored in political science. Before Elizabeth was born, Sandy was quite active politically. She has mentioned a couple of times that if she won the state lottery she would seriously consider running for a political office.

Sandy left college temporarily to stay with her mother when her father died at the age of 45. She was 18 years old and went to work in Wall Street, where she had had summer employment. She was soon put in charge of some mutual funds. She confesses that she was in way over her head, not knowing what she was doing, but she soon learned. She married her mentor, an erratic but successful businessman, whose major ambition was retirement. When he did retire it went against the grain of her work-ethic philosophy. She finished her college education. She and a couple of friends started a sailing venture, her husband joining reluctantly, but left it in the middle of a summer. She then moved out of the house. At the end of the summer, she found herself a job and began to move on. She and her husband lived together for a while again. He started law school. His parents paid his tuition, but she supported him. She wanted children; her husband didn't want the responsibility. She "accidentally" got pregnant, separated, bought herself a co-op, and divorced him after 9 years, when Elizabeth was born. She hired a live-in housekeeper. Her ex-husband never saw the child.

Sandy's second husband, Richard, has two children from his first marriage. He is very involved with his children, and he and Sandy often spend time with them during the week and on weekends. Sandy met Richard nine months after the birth of her daughter. Elizabeth regards him as her father. Both Sandy and Richard are very successful. He is in management. They own a house in New York City and a weekend house by the shore, and have a live-in housekeeper.

Sandy is a short, pretty woman with a serene face and twinkly blue eyes. She has a hilarious sense of humor. She loves to talk, sprinkling anecdotes along the way. She is candid and to the point. She cuts through undue elaborations politely when talking business and gets you to zero in.

Sandy is a striver, according to her husband, and she agrees. She has been on a fast-track career path from the start, except for the year Elizabeth was born. She is the first woman at her level in her organization, managing about 175 people. She earned her MBA while working. She simply sets goals for herself and then goes about implementing them. Someone else may take months or years settling on a house to buy—not Sandy. It is bought, done, and settled within weeks. When she remarried a second child and a weekend house were her goals, quickly achieved.

Sandy is active in her professional organization; she is on the board and chairs a couple of committees. She confines her job to 9–10 hours a day, although she runs a fairly large

toward finishing her degree—he himself has two Ph.Ds. Before Stephen was born, she was an avid tennis player and active in many sports. She is looking forward to getting back to these activities. George is also athletic and active in sports.

Catherine changed her mind about wanting a child when she accidentally became pregnant. Although George didn't want more children, having three grown ones from a previous marriage, he acquiesced. They have a co-op in the city and a house in the country. They have a live-out housekeeper.

Kitty, Vice President, Research Analyst, Brokerage firm. Age, 33. Husband, Peter, about 34, Lawyer. Children, Bridgit, 3 years old; son, just born.

Kitty's parents are of Irish Catholic origin. She is the middle child of 6, 3 brothers and 3 sisters, born within the span of seven years. She believes that this close spacing is the reason why they are such a closely knit family. Her father has a law degree, but he never practiced law; he was in the insurance business. Her mother began to work when the youngest sibling was 5 years old, but only in jobs where she could have the summers off. She organized her life around her children. Eight years later she started to work at a job with a future. She had a high school education only, but worked her way up to a high civil-service position.

Her mother cooked all their meals. She always encouraged the children to bring friends home. "I dont' know how she did it," Kitty says. On Saturdays and Sundays there were often 25 people at dinner. "It didn't faze her at all." They never had any outside help. Her father did a lot too. He diapered, did the Saturday washes, etc. He was "a real pitch-in and do everything guy." There was no defined role for the boys and girls. Everybody was expected to help out.

Kitty speaks of her mother with a great deal of admiration and respect. "What I do is nothing in comparison." "As a role model she really had an impact." Remembering her mothers's leaving for work in the morning, Kitty says, "I thought it exciting and interesting," in comparison with her neighbors where the mothers always stayed at home.

The family jokes about the girls being over-achievers. She herself says that she was always competitive. Her brothers are not as ambitious as the sisters, says Kitty. One brother is a law professor and the other two also teach, one at a college and the other at a well-known private school. One sister is a lawyer; one has a Master of Social Work degree and has four children. "She can't earn enough to afford babysitters," Kitty says.

Kitty is a tall, poised, good looking woman with high cheekbones and a charming smile. She tends to express herself with a drily facetious humor, and she laughs a lot.

Kitty arrived in New York from a nearby state right out of college, where she majored in economics. She was terribly naive, she feels, hardly knew where Wall Street was. That is, nevertheless, where she headed. She advanced herself with "dogged determination" by frequent moves to jobs with better opportunity. "That's the way I was brought up, to do well." She worked in securities all along. After about 6 to 7 years she had a mentor who "pushed her forward" and gave her a good deal of visibility. Kitty emphasizes that in her line of work a mentor is not so important as in corporations, where one needs someone's backing to move up the corporate ladder. She implies that her job requires individual initiative and "knowhow" and that this is the basis for her success. She concedes: "It would have saved a lot of time and effort to have had a mentor earlier in my career." First Vice President is as far as she can go as an analyst. "My success rests upon my stocks going up or down." She expects to move ahead and to continue to earn a sizable income.

Kitty married when she was 25 years old, and they purposely waited to have Bridgit until she was well established in her career. She obtained her MBA while working. She recently started a job where she doesn't have to travel as much as she used to. She mostly manages to confine her job to 9 to 5, although she works late once in a while. She is frequently on TV programs. Her husband is a successful law partner. He is an only child. They own a co-op in the city and a house near the shore. They have a live-out housekeeper. Their second child was born this summer.

The women told me their stories without many questions from me. What specific impact their backgrounds had on their personalities, the development of their careers, and their lifestyles can only be speculated upon without more in-depth study. It is clear, however, from their own statements, that every one of them had experiences that shaped their lives and career orientation.

One thing they all have in common is that they were raised in families where excellence or upward mobility was part of the family ideal, whether stated overtly or not. Thus, logically, they had a common goal, career achievement. They are imbued by the work ethic with which most of them grew up. Each has taken risks and has had mentors; some received more support from theirs than others did.

Here the commonalities appear to end. It is difficult to determine whether any of the mothers of these women fit into the image of the traditional mother, except perhaps Sandy's. Three of the mothers worked outside the home, two of them only when the children had reached school age. Anna's situation is somewhat special because her mother worked in the family business which was just downstairs, so that the mother was available to her and her siblings. However, none of my informants had real experience with nannies taking care of them the way their housekeepers look after their children.

Three of the women state that they had hard-working mothers as role models. Both Karin and Kitty view their mothers as "unusual." Sandy does not mention that her mother worked hard or that she views her as a desirable role model, even though her mother must have led a busy life with six children and was widowed at an early age. Sandy does, however, see her female school principal as a significant role model.

Some other matters of interest are these: Catherine and Karin were the youngest children in the family with a 6- and 7-year span of time between them and their older siblings, and they were given special attention. Sandy was the oldest child, and perhaps special because of it. Hennig and Jardim (1976:99) found that most of the 25 successful female executives who figure in their study were either the oldest child, a child treated as special because of the many years between them and their older siblings, or the only child, or for some other reason treated as such. They also had close relationships with their fathers, as three of my informants seem to have had. The main point Hennig and Jardim make is that the women in their study were treated as "special," thereby building their self-esteem.

Kitty and Anna, however, do not have this kind of place in their family constellation. We do know that Anna's parents worked a small store into a thriving shopping center and thus set examples of people who value success. Her parents were also able to provide education for the girls in the family as well as for the boys. Kitty, a middle child, mentions her own competitiveness; one can easily imagine that she had to compete pretty strenuously for attention in her large family. In addition, her mother was an achiever. Kitty grew up seeing her father and brothers sharing in household responsibilities and child care, an experience which probably affects her expectations of her husband. Catherine's father taught her competitive sports, which may have helped her compete in a male-dominated business.

The precise bearing these circumstances had on my informants' development is not known, but that they did have an effect, I think, few could dispute. Barnett and Baruch

(1978:26) in *The Competent Woman* summarize background characteristics found in several studies of successful women within different professions:

Certain characteristics are common in the background of successful women: being foreign born; having immigrant parents; coming from an affluent family; having one or both parents with high occupational and/or educational status; being an eldest or only child; having no brothers. These characteristics may occur singly or in combination.

They make it clear, of course, that having any of these characteristics in one's background will not guarantee success. It is noteworthy that one or more of them are evident in the backgrounds of all my informants. Being foreign-born is the only characteristic that is not self-explanatory in terms of its possible influence on a person's achievement. The foreign-born women in the study that Barnett and Baruch refer to came from relatively affluent families from Western cultures in which women were well educated and in which neither domestic work nor child care was expected of them; hired help took care of both. In fact, having a professional career was generally the rule or the expectation of these women (Barnett and Baruch 1978:27). All these characteristics apply to Karin's situation, except that her mother took care of her as she was growing up. Anna's family was well-to-do and the girls were well educated, but I don't think the other circumstances mentioned apply. Barnett and Baruch also suggested that many foreign-born women are "less extensively exposed to harmful sex-role stereotyping" (ibid.). I have serious doubts that this may be said of either Anna or Karin.

Finally, my informants all entered the work force during a period of rapidly opening opportunities for women. One may safely infer from their stories that they were well equipped and well positioned to enter the opportunity structure.

Functioning: The "I" vs. The Sustaining Crowd

As widely different as these women are as people, there is something recognizable about them that you quickly sense in the way they talk, the way they manage themselves and their surroundings. It's like recognizing an accent from a different region or another subculture than your own. The first time you wander into the world of successful career women who are mothers as well, especially if your professional life has been spent as a social work psychotherapist and the last decade with one foot in the world of academe, you literally feel you have arrived in a strange country inhabited by very strange people. They even seem to speak a different language. You walk around wide-eyed, asking questions based on experiences from your own subculture which make no sense to them at all. They take pity on you and try to explain, but their language is hard to comprehend. You ask about problems; they stare at you, repeating: "Problems? What problems? There are no problems. Only opportunities." They shake their heads in a bewildered fashion at similarly obtuse questions. "Overwhelmed? What do you mean? You just do it, that's all." You go back to your own world and talk about these strange beings and are told very definitely: "They operate on denial," or whatever other mechanism of defense seems appropriate to the story. You shake your head: "No, you can't apply the same set of rules to them. They're just different from people in our country." Confused and preoccupied, you continue your wanderings, listening, observing, asking your absurd questions, until one day you begin to get the drift.

Seldom do you meet someone there who uses familiar terms such as *problems, feeling frustrated, tired,* etc. And when she speaks, it is in a muffled voice. She is not always happy in the success subculture, because negative language is frowned upon.

My description of the success subculture and of the career women in it is their perception of their world and of themselves as they taught me to understand them. Do they have doubts about their success or questions about their abilities? If any such feelings exist, they are not allowed to surface, or at least they were not conveyed to me.

The women are highly goal-oriented. They talk in terms of three-year, five-year, and ten-year plans. They are very conscious of how they are positioned in their organizations and in their careers; what they can gain in their present positions; where they want to go next; what they can do outside work to gain experience and visibility, such as being on boards of voluntary organizations, making presentations, appearing on TV, and so on. All these activities are part of a definite but flexible plan calculated to further their careers.

They freely acknowledge mistakes. Usually they have already rectified them or are in the process of doing so. Now and then I caught a remark that was critical of some existing behavior. Kitty, for example, remarked at a meeting, "I take my time making decisions," conveying a sense of displeasure with this aspect of herself. This kind of self-criticism concerns areas in which they want to improve, areas that do not fit in with their ideal of themselves and are therefore turned into goals for change. This kind of determination, I think, is an important value to all of them. Their puzzlement with some of my questions was genuine, because the questions implied a lesser expectation of them than they have of themselves.

This is not to say that in soberer moments, when their guards are down, they won't admit to being tired at times; there are difficulties at times, and they do sometimes have concerns. But—and this is a big *but*—the theme is: "It can be handled. There is no sense dwelling on these things. There isn't time."

In meetings of the professional organization advice is freely given and is expected to have a quieting effect on a complainer. (It is also expected that the advice will be heeded.) In private you may note a certain impatience when the conversation turns to a complaint. "It really is so simple. Here's how it can be done," the successful ones seem to say.

It appears that complaining is against the rules. An issue is designated as important or unimportant. If it is important, one can do something about it. Listening to the women, one hears them consciously weighing an issue and making up their minds whether it is worth putting energy into. If they decide it is, it becomes a priority; something they must do, or at least actively try to do. This seems to be another basic rule.

What is considered unimportant is traded off for something more important. They cut corners. Their standards vary considerably. Some women would not be caught dead in clothing that is not immaculate; others find this inconsequential. If the baby spills something on their dress just before they leave for work, they laugh—"So what?"

The complaints heard in both the Career Development and the Working Mothers' meetings are mostly related to husband participation or the lack of it. My informants think that the complainers have either set expectations of their husbands too high or have not figured out strategies to handle them. "Husbands can be trained." There are certain expectations of a husband which a woman would not think reasonable as long as he is responding to "training" and/or is supportive of her. (The expectations, of course, differ, as will be discussed in the next chapter.)

In contrast to their impatience with the complainer, the successful women are quite accepting of someone who asks for support. For example, Sandy is gossiping about Sylvia. She is mimicking and whispering, making fun of everybody, including herself, in the process.

He's going to be a boy and his name is going to be John Smithers Junior. [Sylvia doesn't want to marry the father.] We all certainly know who the father is; there's no need fussing around with that anymore. Here is Sylvia dealing in millions. She was clearly terrified of the whole thing. She's older than me. We had more conversations over things. She approached each thing [with]—"I don't know what I'm doing here. How do I hire someone, Sandy? Just what am I going to do here?"

We sat down. Not to worry: here is a list of people to call, here is a form to interview people. Here are people who just did it. "Should I hire a baby nurse?" Well, here are the pros and cons. We went through everything. . . . Then it was, she went out to buy furniture. She said, "This is awful. It costs hundreds and hundreds of dollars. I can tell he's not going to use this very long." She got that part right. We really are coming of age here because we're trading maternity clothes. That's a real sign of maturity as a mothers' group. One of the elementary things is when we start moving things around. So we matched up baby clothes for her.

Sandy was laughing as she told the story, apparently quite tolerant of this particular kind of inefficiency. The women often mention having talked with a female friend or colleague on the telephone about work or personal issues, exchanging support and advice. It is noteworthy that Sandy's story did not come out of a casual get-together of expectant mothers. It was a meeting to discuss a certain aspect of pregnancy with a newspaper reporter and to have their picture taken for the article.

In sum, there are certain unspoken rules to which the women in the success subculture appear to adhere in their expectation of themselves and of each other. A positive, upbeat approach to career and life is part of their value system. Complaining is unproductive; either one does something to change a situation or one lowers one's expectations. Advice and support are freely given. Too much worry is a waste of energy. The women exert a certain amount of pressure on themselves and others to conform to these standards. They role-model for each other. But the goal is achievement. Achievement vitalizes them, and they are well paid for it to boot. The bottom line is, I think, that they feel in control of their lives.

Thus the atmosphere in the success subculture fosters attitudes of career commitment, optimism, aspiration, self-esteem, and vigor. This phenomenon reminds me of Kanter's (1982:158) assertion that being placed in the opportunity structure of an organization shapes behavior in people so placed that promotes upward mobility.

In interviews, at lunch, in company, and in meetings, these by now not-so-strange beings are quite fun to be with. Their sense of humor is often hilarious, their repartee quick and frequently dry. They all give clear, concise renditions of their lives and family backgrounds with hardly any prompting needed. I have listened to them both in private and on panels. Any topic they are familiar with is presented in a similar fashion. They have strong opinions. Although I have never seen them in action at business meetings, it seems likely that they hold their own with equanimity.

The theme that runs through the women's stories about how they reached their level of achievement is much the same, with some variations: "You work hard. Anyone can make it to where I am, if you don't set up roadblocks on

your way." Some add "luck." Here the individualistic notion, the "I" talking "the language of success," runs head-
on into their intermittent acknowledgment of a contributing,
sustaining crowd throughout the years.

Both Catherine and Sandy are strong proponents of the
"work ethic" theme. Yet Catherine readily concedes how
much she owes her mentor for all he taught her and for his
help in furthering her career. Sandy is more reluctant to
acknowledge that others and circumstances aided her in
achieving her success.

Kitty attributes her success to her determination, and she
views herself as successful by any measure. "I was brought
up that way," she says, "to do well in school. I made a lot
of mistakes, but that made me even more determined. Friends
used to kid me when I was younger, 'Kitty will stop at
nothing to succeed.' " She adds, "And it has nothing to do
with luck."

Karin puts it this way: "I always did what people told me
was impossible." She recounts several "impossible" epi-
sodes in her life and career. "It always worked out well. I
was always very lucky." Karin gives a lot of credit for her
"luck" to her background. Having a father in the diplomatic
service exposed her to more cultures, people, and languages
than most of us ever encounter, and has stood her in good
stead in her line of work. She comes from "old patrician
families" on both her mother's and her father's side. She
thinks her background gave her advantages. She views her
mother as "unusual" and "not traditional." In addition, she
believes that she often happened to be in the right place at
the right time, which enabled her to take advantage of opportunities.

Anna thinks her success came from "a lot of hard work
and luck. I was in the right place when the right openings
came about." She expands a bit: "It is much more difficult
to get the job than to do the job, and you need luck to get
into the slot. Once you are there and you have the basic

tools, have the education and the technical competence, you can do it most of the time." Anna is really describing here the entry into the opportunity structure. She continues:

It's very important to know how to deal with people. I have seen many people fail at really important jobs because, over the years, they have made too many enemies. That's not to say that there isn't a bunch of people that do not like me, but I try to get along. I try to develop contacts.

Anna describes how she consciously makes efforts to meet new people and to introduce herself to different kinds of people when she is at professional meetings. She is pleased that so many people have heard about her. That's because "I have been here for so many years—the fact that I've been in the company for ten years and I've worked in so many areas and for so many people who have moved to big, influential jobs." They think of her when something comes up, such as a call I had just overheard her taking, a call from a major university to give a one-day seminar. Her former boss had suggested her. She is clearly in the opportunity structure, in which, Kanter (1982:247) contends, she belongs to "a class of advantaged persons who are offered the prospects for increasing their opportunities and power."

The women's statements reflect the varying degrees to which they acknowledge, if they do at all, that a multitude of contributing factors and circumstances enabled them to arrive at where they are today. One woman in the pilot study went to one extreme in denying any role for a sustaining crowd in her success, "I would like to think I would have done everything if in a vacuum. I would have set up conditions or created an environment for it to have happened." She negates what applies to all of them: the times and the family they were born into, the color of their skin, their socialization process, the personality characteristics evolving from it as well as resources such as intelligence, education, and position in the social structure, which enabled them to gain entry via networks and mentors into the opportunity structure, which in turn enabled them to move to the positions they now are in. Thus, in their conversations about their success, there is a real ambivalence about acknowledging the role of the sustaining crowd versus the "I." Sometimes they deny it any role at all.

This individualistic attitude probably has something to do with most of the women's avoidance of the feminist label. Baruch, Barnett, and Rivers (1983:237–38) believe individualism—deeply ingrained in the American culture—to be the reason why the women in their comprehensive survey view their current well-being more in personal than in sociopolitical terms and see the women's movement as having little impact on them personally. Many of the women I met during my research give a good deal of recognition to the positive effect the women's movement has had on women's opportunities, but to identify themselves as feminists seems almost repugnant to some. (Karin is an exception.) Yet, they stand for equality with men in the job market and in the home; they are for an Equal Rights Amendment and other feminist issues. I believe that they fear the connotation of extremism which society and apparently they themselves often tend to attach to feminism and how, in turn, the label can be used against them in a hostile work environment.

Karin and Anna's partial attribution of their success to luck is probably left over from traditional attitudes on their part, although Karin rightly accredits some of her success to her parents and her background. Barnett and Baruch (1978:26) in *The Competent Woman* cite several studies of men's and women's attitude toward achievement. The overall conclusion was that women tended to think a task must have been easy or luck was on their side if they were successful, while men credited their own ability.

At present, only Sandy is in a line position. There is no question in her mind that she will become the chief executive officer and/or chair the board of a financial institution one day. She was always rated among the top 10 percent managerially and moved on the fast track wherever she worked. Sandy is the only one of my informants who has a large staff to manage, about 175 people. Anna has the opportunity to move into ever-increasing responsibility within the staff areas of her firm. She can also, if she chooses, move into a line position. Karin has had accelerated promotions and is now two steps away from the top level within her organization. If a woman will be allowed into the top executive spot, she has a chance. In Kitty's and Catherine's particular line of work, there is only one more step—Chief Research Analyst. Catherine, I believe, could also set her sights on a partnership. At present there are only male partners in her company, and she is not interested, at the moment, in investing the amount of time attaining a partnership would require. But there are other opportunities. It is important for both Kitty and Catherine to be visible—for their reputations and earning power. They appear on TV programs and are quoted in the newspapers. They already have solid earning capacities.

With this kind of track record, most of the women feel they can do anything they set their minds to. They exude so much confidence that one is always hard put not to believe wholeheartedly that they can reach any goal they want. Kotter (1982:142) believes that the "I Can Do Anything" syndrome which they manifest is a dangerous "disease," one that afflicts only the strong and the successful. He concludes in his study of 15 male general managers that if they tried "to do something in a very different and inappropriate environment," it could be fatal. Like my informants, his managers had never experienced failure because they had worked in the same familiar settings and/or industries for most of their careers and had gathered extensive knowledge, experience, and contacts, which, Kotter maintains, are essential ingredients of their success. However, he fails to include the support their present families afford them. The general managers believed they could transfer their skills anywhere, ignoring the enormous support systems that surrounded them. That the "I" cannot succeed without a sustaining crowd is not quite the way Kotter puts it but is nevertheless what his data imply.

The women say that they are in fine physical condition. A friend of Sandy's told me that Sandy has been quite sick several times but likes to ignore her illnesses as much as possible. Her husband comments, "Three minutes after she has gotten over being sick, she has forgotten she was." Karin tends to have respiratory illnesses but tries to ignore her "colds." They are a waste of precious time. Kitty was annoyed that she didn't have an overabundance of energy while she was pregnant. Otherwise she is healthy. Catherine is never sick. Anna has had a great many problems around her pregnancies and miscarried once, but otherwise she too is in very good health.

Many of the other women I met during my research remarked on their good health and rich fund of energy. The busy female attorneys in Epstein's (1981:325) study also describe themselves as healthy, with high energy levels. High energy and good health appear to go together in the case of the successful career woman. Well-being can be added to these assets according to one of the key findings in Baruch, Barnett, and Rivers' (1983:43) extensive study of women; married women in high-prestige jobs who had children— similar to the women in my study—scored highest on all their indices of well-being.

The usual assumption about these women is that with their several roles and all their activity they must be worn-out. This belief is based on the traditional concept of energy which presumes that there is only a fixed amount available to a person and each activity undertaken reduces that amount. This concept does not hold true for the women described here, nor does it hold true for men in high-powered jobs, and it is challenged by several researchers. Their findings show that there is a group of people whose energy is not reduced by a lot of activity.

Sieber (1974:567–78) asserts that "the benefits of role accumulation tend to outweigh any stress to which it might give rise, thereby yielding net gratification." In essence, Sieber argues that role multiplicity, rather than overwhelm a person, may give him/her more security and autonomy, more self-esteem and flexibility of functioning. These benefits are seen in one form or another in the career women's lives and functioning as discussed throughout this book. The rewards are an integral part of the opportunity structure to which my informants belong.

Marks (1977:921–36) challenges the "scarcity" approach to measuring human energy or the "spending" or "drain" theory that "sociologists generally invoke." He suggests an energy-creation theory of multiple roles; that is, energy is created by the satisfaction of a job well done and the rewards attendant to such an accomplishment. Baruch, Barnett, and Rivers (1983) call this the "recharge your battery" model. Marks points out that empirical evidence only partly supports the "drain" theory, i.e., the minority of multiple role players whose energy is not drained are not addressed by the theory (Marks 1977:925). He further reminds us that human physiology implies that under normal circumstances people "have abundant and perpetually renewing resources" of energy (1977:926–27).

He posits that in our culture people implicitly decide how to use their energy and whose demands will be honored, if anyone's. People may channel their energy to those activities "that are the most greedily demanded and heavily sanctioned or those activities that are simply the most valued culturally and personally." People with multiple roles can determine in which role or roles they will invest energy. If there is a feeling of loss of energy, it is due to the *stance* of people toward the particular activity-cluster or their role partners within them. Marks believes that we find abundant energy "for anything to which we are highly committed, and we often feel more energetic after having done it." Doing something to which we are uncommitted leaves us feeling spent (1977:927). He stresses that "particular types of commitment systems are responsible for whether or not strain will occur" (1977:921). This view corresponds with the psychological one of psychic energy being released only in favor of actions which are in line with a person's values, wishes, and goals. The issue of commitment will be discussed later in this chapter.

The women I got to know well are all firmly established in their careers. They also have very young children. For these two reasons they have managed to carve out relatively set schedules for themselves. A couple of the women travel occasionally, but not extensively. They sometimes take work home, but most find that staying late at the office is a more efficient way of finishing their work when pressure is on. Some think that they pack more into an office day than their male colleagues because the men have more leeway in terms of time. The women cannot procrastinate. They need to be superefficient at all times. The one thing none of them have is time for themselves.

All my informants state that their careers have been slowed down by their having children. They strongly feel that if brakes are put on their careers, it should be at their own choice. Anna and Sandy, especially, had their careers slowed. Anna decided to gamble with her career in order to have a child. She estimates that it slowed her down about two years in her career progression. The first time Sandy was pregnant, she was put to pasture for about a year by her female boss. Sandy has not quite forgiven her for that treatment, although in hindsight she grudgingly admits that even though she missed out on a promotion she had been groomed for, it was probably for the best. No one could have foreseen that her daughter would have a condition that required her being in traction in the hospital for ten days as an infant and then for months in a body cast which had to be changed as the baby grew. She was in a harness for a long time afterwards. Sandy does not want to dwell on the subject. She had separated from her first husband before the baby was born.

Kitty states: "I could have moved forward more rapidly had I not had the baby three years ago. [Her second child was recently born.] People around me don't think I have slowed down, but I know I have. I just haven't been as focused on moving on, because there were other things."

Catherine says,

I have moved ahead, of course. I do spend less time at work and more with my child. I do regard my career less aggressively than a man in my position, so I haven't moved ahead as a man might have. That's partly coming from me and not necessarily from them. There are a lot of other things in life that interest me. Maybe that's because I am a woman. I don't know. I love my career and I am happy, but I am also not going to work twelve hours a day.

She is going at her own pace. She tells of her boss, who remarked on his wedding anniversary: "It's been eighteen years now and perhaps [the equivalent of] four of them were spent at home." The rest were spent at work and in business travel. "I don't want that kind of life," says Catherine emphatically.

Every successful career woman and mother I meet agrees that it is very important to establish oneself in a career before having a child. The reasons given for late pregnancy are: first, that a woman can then afford the kinds of things related to child care, such as a housekeeper. Second, by the time she is established, everybody knows she is serious about her career. She is no longer "proving herself," which means no letting up, no deviance in time spent at the office. That could seriously hamper her career. Third, the mere fact that she is in an upper-echelon position entitles her to flexibility of time. She can disappear from the office for a visit with her child's pediatrician or run to school for her child's performance in a play, can leave briefly in an emergency. All my informants have stories about such occurrences. Everybody knows that they will get their work done somehow, and they do.

Jean, in the pilot study, is career-focused, has two young children, one an infant, and works 75 hours a week. She says, "Superwoman? Only if you are on the outside. If inside, you are being matched hour by the hour by men on the right and women on the left. That's what it is. It's like flying with the rest. If you want to be up there, that's it." She travels a lot, but adds that many travel more than she.

Jean had a child (not planned) early in her career but didn't stop to breathe, didn't want to slow down her momentum. Although it put her in the red financially—to have a live-in housekeeper and she had to do without other things she wanted—she viewed going into debt and doing without things as an investment for the future. Karin, with very little time between pregnancies, in some ways is in a similar situation, although she was established in her career when she had her children. Her husband is still in school, but because she wanted to beat the "biological clock," she has had to forgo some of the things the others now take for granted. The amount of energy she has to expend to stay on top of her job and keep her family going she tolerates by telling herself (and me): "It's not going to last forever, so why worry about it?" Her doctor, however, tells her she should take better care of herself.

Some of the concessions that my informants have made to their families, such as curtailing working hours as much as feasible, limiting travel, etc., are paralleled in a 1980 follow-up of a 1970 study of dual-career couples (Poloma, Pendleton, and Garland 1982:184). The career women in that study felt that being limited graphically was a cost to their careers. Otherwise their work patterns, like those of my informants, resembled those of many male colleagues. "Almost without exceptions married professional women with children found it necessary to compromise some of the 'extras' of professional demands because of the family," i.e., evening work, travel, annual meetings, etc. (1982:184). Neither my informants nor any of the women I met during my research mentioned that they had lost out on any opportunities because they were restricted to New York by family responsibilities. Missing of opportunities may very well have occurred; the subject simply did not come up.

There is a whole range of value systems related to the career within the women's world of success, from heavily career oriented to a more family-focused approach, depending on how fast and how far they want to move up the ladder. As can be seen, each choses her own path.

The women never question their right to realize their potential just as men do or are expected to do. The idea of realizing themselves only through caring for husbands and children is utterly foreign to them, even though they were brought up in a time when this was the predominant pattern for women. But my informants came into the work force in the wake of the civil rights movement and the women's movement, when women were beginning to accept that it was morally right to care for themselves (Gilligan 1982:149). (Many women, I grant, had accepted this long ago, but they were in a fairly small minority.) Opportunities for women were also opening up at a relatively rapid rate, and societal attitudes toward working women were becoming more tolerant.

The wave of research that has taken place in the last decade or two finds the traditional psychology of women and the old sex-role expectations much in need of revision because both were shaped by the perceptions of men. Gilligan (1982), in particular, points this out. Miller (1976:40,61), in *Toward a New Psychology of Women*, holds that for women to help other people grow while ignoring their own development is constricting and debilitating. She asserts that realizing oneself and being connected with others are not mutually exclusive but, instead, a freeing experience for oneself and for those with whom one is affiliated (1976:116). The women described in these pages seem to have intuitively made Miller's concept their own.

Like most women, women in the success subculture want equality with men in opportunities and in pay. In connection with these two issues, the present debate is frequently focused on motherhood and working, motherhood often being used as a weapon against equality in the workplace. The women feel that they often have to prove themselves by performing better than their male colleagues, perhaps especially so if they are mothers. Only recently, according to Sandy, have they begun to "come out of the closet" as mothers, that is, have pictures of their children in their offices, share stories at work about their children, and so on. Earlier they had felt that to display motherhood might make them suspect as serious professional women, and had played it down because of sexist attitudes and discrimination they had encountered. They will not allow themselves any behavior that can be used to downgrade their abilities.

Karin relates two stories that illustrate her concern not to let her boss or her colleagues think that being a mother will interfere with her work. She found that when she became a mother and did not always stick to her scheduled arrival and departure time at work, the men would use her as an excuse for being late or leaving early. She changed that by being on time and leaving on time. The men soon started coming in and leaving as they used to and stopped using her as an excuse.

Another time, her boss suddenly called a meeting when she had a pediatrician's appointment with Lise. Rather than tell the boss, she sent her secretary by taxi to be with Lise and her housekeeper until she herself arrived. Her secretary then went back to the office. Karin said that if the meeting had dragged on, she would have told her boss she had to leave and why.

If sexist attitudes stand in their way, the women will seek ways to deal with them; otherwise they ignore them. "What can you do? Clobber them over the head?" Not that they don't poke fun at the men.

A panel member tells a story at a meeting:

When I got married, having worked in the department for three years, the manager came over to me and said, "All right, when are you going to quit?" I was shocked. I hadn't given any indication, but I realized [then that] there wasn't one guy in the department whose wife works. I had never worked in a department like that before. But all these guys, their wives either work until they have a child or they quit. There just is a pattern and it's going to be uphill all the way.

She was responding to a question as to whether the panel members thought there had been any backsliding in recent years in women's gains in the business world. The panel member was comparing her industry to others, such as finance, where women have generally been more accepted. She went on to say:

I don't know if it's backsliding. The old boys' network has worked for some women I know, whose fathers are well placed and [had] gotten their daughters in somewhere. That's not backsliding then. I don't see any emphasis anymore to make sure you are interviewing women. I don't see any women coming into my department, and it's not for lack of applicants.

There was a consensus among the panel members that things were standing still, not backsliding; there was no forward momentum as there had been in the Carter Administration.

They spoke with sardonic humor about the men entrenched in senior positions in the traditional corporate world. The same panel member commented again:

In my particular industry, there definitely is a bias. Most of the people in upper management are right now about age 50. A lot of these men treat anyone, any female, including the Corporate Secretary, a lawyer who is very well known, she must be in her fifties, and they treat her as if she was their daughter. That attitude you can't break by being more executive.

After some more interchanges, she added, "Most of the people who make it to the top in most corporations sit there and slug it out year after year. Rarely do you see a 40-year-old guy up there. Most of the time it is a 60-year-old person who is succeeding a 62-year-old guy. That person has just physically outlasted everybody for that job" (laughter).

Some of the women estimated that for the next 10 to 15 years it will be extremely difficult for women to get into senior executive positions in the corporate world, until the old-timers have disappeared from the scene. The "pool of brains" is increasing, and competition is getting tougher. A few members wondered if, by that time, the younger women would not get into the top positions instead of them. One woman said firmly that they wouldn't let that happen, that the younger women would have to wait their turn. One could visualize battle formations taking shape: the group of men in one; the present age group of women in the second; the younger women forming the third. They are all marching toward the precious few senior executive positions available. The battle could be bloody.

There was an agreement that moving to smaller corporations or starting their own firms would be the best way to achieve their goal of becoming top executives.

Jean, in a pilot study interview, compared the attitudes in a previous job she had, where everyone from the secretaries up to senior-level people asked when she was pregnant with her first child, "What are you going to do?" "Are you going to quit?" "Are you staying?" "Here," she continued, "no one, *no* one asked me, not even when I was leaving or returning. The assumption was at this point that

I was just going to have a baby. [She was now pregnant with her second child.] I rather think that [that] I was married and a mother was a plus here, meant well-rounded, having more experience."

Sandy tells of difficult politics going on at the office, "real trouble," she says, which probably won't be settled for months. Her boss suddenly dropped the serious subject they are discussing and commented, "I am so glad you are pregnant." Sandy thought this a rather strange remark until her boss concluded, "That will keep you here for a while." "Oh, not that again," she groaned inwardly, remembering having been shelved with her first pregnancy. She doesn't really mind not moving on right now, she says. There are more people around this time who want to participate in the event, that is, her second husband and her daughter. When her son is born will be time enough to think about the next step in her career.

What has been described so far in this chapter are some glimpses of the successful women's philosophies of life—how they view themselves, their careers, and their world. We have seen a subculture in which the inhabitants are highly committed to their careers, highly goal-oriented, high achievers, and hard workers. Certain behaviors attendant to these attitudes are expected of the inhabitants; they should be upbeat, optimistic, highly self-confident, energetic, assertive, articulate, and strong believers in improving themselves. They are supportive of those who adhere to these behaviors and less tolerant of those who do not. You may deviate in other areas as long as you conform to the list above. The women are generally in good health. Each has her particular brand of humor, and they are great fun to be with. They are ambivalent about acknowledging that they were aided along the way to success. They wait until they are established in their careers to have children; and for many, children have meant a temporary slowdown in their career progression.

These women are unquestionably in the opportunity structure of the organizational and societal hierarchy and moving upward each at her idiosyncratic pace. The top tiers of the pyramid, however, are at present closed to women.

Many of the personality characteristics outlined above accord with those that Burke (1982:237–45) describes in his article on "Leaders: Their Behavior and Development." I do consider my informants leaders. They are often the first women in their high-echelon jobs. They can be found on TV and in other forums, actively chairing committees in business and professional organizations, charities, and so on.

To paraphrase Burke on leaders: They are brighter than most, have above-average ambition. They like influencing others. They are autonomous and have a strong sense of being in control of their lives. They enjoy organized work and are not necessarily interested in popularity. Burke also listed androgyny as a personality quality to look for in leaders (1982:244). I prefer not to include this, since it depends on stereotypical ideas of female and male qualities. I am not alone in finding problems with androgyny. Warren (1982:170–86) holds that "androgyny is useful to conceptualize the process of overcoming sex role stereotyping, at both the individual and the social level." She hopes, however, that the word will soon become obsolete. Beardsley (1982) sees androgyny as an obstacle to overcoming stereotypes. She argues, "Part of the problem with androgyny is that it fosters the tendency to dichotomize in general, so that not only are humans classified as 'masculine' and 'feminine,' but also as 'rational' and 'intuitive/empathetic,' 'aggressive' and 'submissive,' or whatever" (1982:170).

Gilligan (1982) found in her study that women through their psychological development process are more concerned with people and the effect moral decision-making has on others than most men are. Such concern lends itself to a more participatory management style, which is currently debated in the business community and largely favored. Peters and Waterman (1982), for example, are proponents of this kind of management style in their bestselling book, *In Search of Excellence*. This style is quite relevant to my informants' interaction and management of their social system because, as we shall see in later chapters, they do show concern for their present sustaining crowd.

Kotter (1982:36) added a few points that would also apply to my informants: he found the general managers even in temperament, personable, and good at developing relationships with people. In addition, there are some skills which seem vital for my informants. They have highly developed organizational skills. Every one has devised a way of keeping track of her schedule for the day, week, and month; the busier they are, the more complex their system. Secretaries are invaluable in this area, sometimes coordinating their schedules, reminding them of appointments, having materials ready for them, making certain everybody is attending meetings, making lunch and dinner reservations, ordering taxis, etc.—much the same work, of course, that a male executive would have his secretary do. One woman gets a card each morning from her secretary showing all her appointments, where, when, and what is on the agenda, personal and business; and it is often updated during the day. There is a separate list of all the things that have to be done that day. What doesn't get done is rescheduled. Telephone calls, in and out, tracked by name and number. Some of the women keep track themselves, and some have separate lists for weekend houses—what to take and so on.

A great deal of minutia is delegated to the secretary, relieving the executive woman of worry about details and keeping her on track. In addition, one secretary also handles the details and correspondence for her boss's outside committee work and other personal matters. Others may do telephoning and personal correspondence, including typing course papers for school. Practically all the secretaries have baby-sat for the women at some point or other, when the child had to be brought to the office in an emergency, such as a sick housekeeper.

The women's justifications for using their secretaries in non-job-related ways are varied. One woman considered it demeaning to her secretary to be used for personal matters and tried to limit this to a minimum, but did concede that her secretary had baby-sat for her child in the office in an emergency. Mostly the women rationalize such use of secretaries by doing things for them in return. For example, they may be accommodating about schedules, let secretaries take care of their own personal problems, i.e., an emergency doctor's appointment during office hours for their children or themselves, and be personally friendly. One secretary told me she had no objection to handling some of her boss's personal affairs because she was paid better than the other secretaries and had been given more power in the office. She was also invited to management seminars, etc. One secretary, although not stating it outright, indicated that she disliked and tried to distance herself from such requests.

The career women surround themselves with capable people in whom they have explicit trust. That is one of the keys to their success. Things are delegated, especially what they consider boring or detailed work that can be done as well, if not better, by people around them. What is important to one may not be to another. Karin, for instance, is the only one of my informants who gives her 2-year-old a bath. All the others delegate this task to their housekeepers, on weekdays at least. One could, of course, cite many other examples of how they differ in their choice of priorities.

The delegation of work, a managerial skill, is the primary strategy in their management of their various roles in their social system, a privilege they have through their position in the hierarchy. This cuts down their work to a manageable level. Actually, in this regard they are much better off than the housewife, who generally has no one to delegate work to. Baruch, Barnett, and Rivers (1983:145) found that work was often a buffer against stress of family and childcare responsibilities. Women felt better able to say no to excessive demands for doing things if they worked. They also thought they had more perspective, and minor concerns didn't loom so large.

Another important skill the women have learned is to compartmentalize, i.e., they are able to focus on the present and tune out other areas of their lives. Their sustaining crowd says, "she is all there" with the subject at hand. They focus on the child when with the child, on work when at work, and so on, thus preventing one role from interfering with another. This is an invaluable ability. Kitty comments,

The key thing is to walk out the door and leave it [pressure] behind you. You are dealing with the stock market, which is a major unknown. I have a real ability to do that—concentrate on one thing at a time. Once I leave, between 5 P.M. and 9 in the morning there is nothing I can do. If a stock is going down, the clients are going through the roof and the brokers are all screaming at you. There is really nothing you can do, so I just close that off, but it has taken me years to develop that ability.

Apart from possessing certain personality qualities, then, there are skills the women learn to make life easier for themselves in handling their various roles. They are happy to share helpful techniques and strategies with each other, as they did at the Career Development meetings.

The strategic significance for the women of belonging to the success subculture should not be underestimated, in my opinion. Being surrounded by people similar to them, and as ambitious as they are, they have powerful support systems around them, where they do not see themselves as deviant or different. These support systems afford them a certain insulation from their critics. This is a very different situation from that faced by the successful female executives of their mothers' generation (Hennig and Jardim 1976). They were isolated, and they did not have each other as role models.

Thus the professional organization, which is an integral part of the success subculture, has a dual purpose, both facilitating their career goals and providing a network where they find people they can measure themselves against and fashion themselves after, who will support them and spur them on. Sandy provides two excellent examples of these functions at two different occasions. At a Career Development meeting Sandy states:

[This organization] gives you a second peer group. If you were always comparing yourself with people at work or the crowd you graduated with, this is rather a different set. I think in most cases where you are dealing on boards, whether [this organization] or something else, you tend to deal with higher achievers. When I sit in an [association] meeting, I always feel like a slouch. There is no question about it, I'm not doing anything in comparison to the rest of the crowd.

To her the meeting is a stimulus to do more.

Sandy furnishes another example. When she was pregnant and separated from her first husband, one of her dynamo organization friends asked her, "Sandy, have you finished your MBA yet? You know we need your name for the pool of people eligible for board membership." "That really made sense to me, I went and got it. Not to please her, but myself." (Shorthand for not allowing herself to sit around feeling sorry for herself; that would be a waste of time.) "It was very supportive," adds Sandy. Apropos of this example, Epstein (1981:325) notes that women attorneys, apart from being extremely efficient time-users, also use work as a means of obtaining "relief from personal trouble . . . rather than letting it deflect from work."

The women are helpful to each other in other areas as well. At the Working Mothers' luncheons, for example, it was notable that one often met women who were considering having a child. They were there to find out how their colleagues with children were faring. They clearly felt that the meetings were helpful to them in making up their minds about what to do. One woman who became a regular told me that she shared all the information she gathered at the luncheons with her husband.

So the Working Mothers group fulfills a third purpose, namely, emotional and tangible support in listening to each other's concerns, sharing one's own experiences, and giving concrete tips on resources such as the names of available housekeepers, babysitters, and so on. The group furnishes forms to fill out on such people, and many have obtained help through this informal resource. Kitty, for example, recently got her new housekeeper this way, a sister of another member's housekeeper.

The women are the hub, general managers and members of the board who develop strategies to run the family in a way that frees sufficient time for them to devote to their careers. Thus the career is the core department around which the family department has to adjust. Sometimes strategies are developed in conjunction with another member of the board (husband), who frequently functions also as administrative assistant. However, the daily running of the household is almost exclusively in the women's hands. To sum up, the strategies they use to keep their social system working are to plan, to delegate tasks and responsibilities, to instruct in regard to these, to surround themselves with competent people whom they can trust and use to do the work they cannot or do not want to do themselves, to lower standards in some areas, such as housecleaning and meal preparation (this particular strategy will be discussed more fully later), to compartmentalize in order to keep one role from interfering with another, and finally to see to it that the reward systems are adequate for the people involved, including themselves.

By implementing these strategies, the women can be away from home for long periods of time. In fact, hypothetically,

3

The Husbands

Is there a man behind every successful woman? In listening to and observing my informants, it seemed to me that the whole scheme of things would be wrong for each one of them without a husband in the picture. I believe that the women either consciously or unconsciously think that a relationship with a man and a child will complete the cycle of their success. Gilligan (1982:127) writes:

As the events of women's lives and of history intersect with their feelings and thought, a concern with individual survival comes to be branded as "selfish" and to be counterposed to the "responsibility" of a life lived in relationships. And in turn, responsibility becomes, in its conventional interpretation, confused with responsiveness to others that impedes a recognition of self. The truths of relationship, however, return in the rediscovery of connection, in the realization that self and other are interdependent and that life, however valuable in itself, can only be sustained by care in relationships.

Sandy is a good example of the need for a relationship, although she functioned on a high level when she had no husband. Despite having a sick child and going to school at night, she continued to be successful in her work. In less than nine months, however, she became involved with Richard.

Epstein (1981:342) observes in *Women in Law* that

Managing marriage and a professional career is assumed to be hard on women and on both their marriages and careers. Gate-keepers [men in the upper echelons of business and the professions] like to attribute women's failure to attain top-ranking positions to their marital obligations. Yet, one of our strongest findings was that women who achieve unusual success are more likely to be married than single.

It has already been noted that Baruch, Barnett, and Rivers (1983:143) found that women who were married, had children, and were in high-prestige jobs scored the highest of all the women in their survey on all the indices of well-being. Their and Epstein's findings indicate that being married can be highly beneficial for the successful career woman.

Let's look now at the husbands and how they function.

The husbands of my informants are in their thirties and early forties except for Catherine's husband George, who is about 57. They are all successful in their fields. Andre is the only one not established yet; he is finishing his graduate education.

All appear to be totally accepting of their wives having careers. Three of them had working mothers: one's mother helped out in the father's business, another was a secretary, and a third was a registered nurse, so that a woman working outside the home was not foreign to them. Otherwise their mothers all carried out the traditional role of rearing the children, looking after the household, cooking, etc. Their fathers participated little if at all in such tasks. On the whole the picture one gets, however much the mother worked outside the home, is that the fathers played the traditional role of the breadwinner who should do only "men's work" and be catered to.

I have the distinct impression that, in most instances, my informants' wishes and plans are implemented. Sandy and Kitty took the initiative in buying a weekend house, for example. Kitty's husband Peter initially did not want a house;

now he sees it as an investment. Kitty tells of the house-hunting; "One weekend I announced I was going to drive up to look at houses. I hoped that he would come [laughing], and he did." Sandy had informed Richard before they married that a weekend house was among her plans, as was a second child. Both her goals have been accomplished. Catherine, when she accidently became pregnant, wanted the child; George did not. Her wish prevailed. George appears to be the only one to have set conditions. It is Catherine's job to take responsibility for the child, which she has accepted, although George clearly helps out more than he is willing to acknowledge. On the whole the women's strong wills seems to set the tone for the marriage, and their goals appear to be the predominant ones in the marriage. They all, however, make concessions to their husbands in some form.

My informants' husbands seem to have both respect and admiration for their wives' successful careers. The wives, in turn, take it for granted that their husbands accept them as career women. I feel fairly certain that they wouldn't have married them otherwise. Jean (pilot study) comments, "I married a guy who knew what package he was buying and accepted the terms. I think his reaction [would be that] I would fall short to do anything less. He wouldn't want me to stop working at this point."

Richard laughingly tells a story about having expressed his disapproval of Sandy's mentioning him by name in a newspaper interview. She told him, "You knew you weren't marrying a shy, retiring type." "She was absolutely right," remarks Richard. Sandy added, "That was not in any contract, not implied, not perceived. You can't say that." Richard responds with more laughter, "True, there is a general support. We both from a work point of view have a very good understanding of the frustrations we have at work. That's very good."

At another point Richard remarks:

We handle our staff very similarly, always one more push to get people to go beyond themselves [as is true with themselves]— Sandy, because she sees another opportunity at the end of the rainbow, I, because the wolves are snapping at my heels. That's my insecurity. . . . Sandy is what my mother describes as a striver, and it's Sandy's view that you go and you do things, which is very good for me, because my general view is, I want them, but if it requires an extension of energy, I probably won't do it.

Sandy listens and agrees emphatically.

Catherine's husband encourages and pushes her to finish her doctoral degree. She explains that the degree will make her more marketable if the economy should go sour and she has to look for another job. It seems like a remote possibility. They are both successful, but nothing is left to chance. George is also twenty years older than she, which may have something to do with his wanting to see her secure financially, even though she confesses that she hates to study. Also, George himself has two Ph.D's. He proudly shows to their friends clippings from newspapers where she has been quoted.

Andre gave up almost two years by going with Karin to an important post, where he had no chance of advancing himself but where she could further her career. He likes independent, energetic women and cannot conceive of being married to someone who wants to be a housewife exclusively. "I don't think we would have married each other if he hadn't felt this way," comments Karin. His mother worked as a nurse. Before having children, he had thought it a good idea for Karin to stay home for a year after their children were born. He changed his mind when Lise was born and Karin was home on maternity leave. He wondered how she could take it, being home all the time, and thoroughly approved of her returning to work.

Anna told me that Robert wanted her to quit working early in her career when she was unhappy with the jobs she had. Robert broke in, "I made enough money. But that was so many years ago." She teasingly said to him when I was visiting, "I haven't heard that suggestion ever since I started bringing in money." Anna doesn't think that Robert really comprehends what it means to work in the corporate world. He never has to work overtime. He doesn't understand how she can get overloaded with work at times, how this is expected of her. He complains about it.

Peter apparently was also clear about the kind of marriage he was getting into. Kitty always knew she wanted to work. She wouldn't dream of just staying at home. It bored her to death to stay home a few weeks after her first child was born. Peter, an only child, comes from a very traditional home. His mother did not work outside the home and, according to Kitty, catered to her husband's and son's every need. Of all the husbands he seems to have had to adjust the most to a very different family arrangement from the one he grew up in. He maintains, however, that everything has evolved very much the way he had envisioned it.

All the husbands help out in some way with household and child responsibilities, but they do not share equally with their wives, and the overall responsibility is left to the women. My informants seem to accept this as inevitable and do not express any resentment.

Epstein (1981) in *Women in Law* sees a greater participation over the years in child care among the younger husbands and some of the older ones: "Yet, in all cases I have seen or heard reported, it is clear that it is the mother who is primarily responsible for the baby, by choice, agreement, or simply *de facto*, with the father acting as an interested and proud partner" (1981:375–76).

Listening to other women at meetings can teach one a good deal about the wives' strategies to get husbands to participate. Many of the men, according to the women, feel they share at least 50/50. Most of the women do not agree with this estimate. Some say, "We both think we do 75 percent of the work." The husbands really think that they share or do more than their wives. It seems to boil down to the fact that the man is not cognizant of the planning involved in having everything run smoothly. The women have to remember endless details, such as the need for a babysitter or the planning of a menu. I am certain there are exceptions in some of these areas, but the women have the overall management role when it comes to child care and running the household.

At least two meetings I attended contained extensive discussions of husband participation. The consensus is that "husbands are trainable." Leaving things undone is one of the major strategies to get husbands to participate in conjunction with this credo. It seems more common than discussion and negotiation. Sometimes a declaration is made to the husbands about an expectation. This way the women avoid constantly requesting participation and above all asking for help, which they do not consider a good idea. "We went into this marriage, both working, and we did it together. We are partners."

How they handle the training of husbands comes out vividly both in the women's meetings and in the visits with husbands and wives together, as well as in interviews with individual women. They sound rather benevolent most of the time, but they are quite candid about their expectations and they do have strong opinions about them.

A pregnant woman talks about life with her husband to delighted recognition and laughter from the rest of the women at a meeting:

It is a matter of training. I learned it on my first management job at work. A lot of my problem was not delegating, not taking time to teach—things my husband didn't want to do, like cleaning the bathroom. He really didn't know how to do it, organize around it. He didn't know about products. It may sound ridiculous, but you have to take time to explain. He didn't know you don't clean the bathroom floor with Clorox. He had no idea you have to sort the laundry, and the man is in his thirties. He always took his laundry out before we married. His mother never had him do things. She waited on the men hand and foot. Cooking, for example. When he went back to school for two years, I continued working. I bought him *The Sixty-Minute Gourmet* and told him, "I'm not going to cook now. I can't leave work to come home and cook." He just took to it, started with the first recipe and worked his way through. [Roars of laughter.] That's the way he does things, methodically. He didn't know how to cook. Now he does.

A woman at the meeting who obviously hadn't gotten the message wanted her husband to take the initiative in cleaning things up, straightening things out. She said it was as if he walked around with blinders. Responses to this were: "It has to do with training." "We're just asking for it when we say, 'Gee, will you help me out?' I don't buy that at all." "It is not my house. It's our house. It is not mother's work. It's parents' work." The woman ignores the comments and goes on to say her husband wants a second child. But she is not going through that again. She has to do almost everything herself, although he thinks he helps. "Maybe," she says, "I am a little crazy. I just do the things that need to be done. People tell me 'have someone do the cleaning for you.' 'You shouldn't make such meals. Go out and buy them.'" She feels she should be good at everything. Someone lowers the boom: "I hear your accommodating point of view and I can see why, peace at any price sort of thing. I don't adhere, myself, to that school." She goes on to tell a story about an experience of her own:

I had left the wastepaper basket in the hallway and Dick kept walking past it. I commented on that to Judy, whom I was talking to on the phone, and she said, "Oh, Jean, he is so wonderful. How can you even complain?" and I said, "You're right." As I thought about it the next 45 minutes, I went into a slow burn. I called her back and said, "You have got that all wrong. I get a large green check. It goes right into the bank from the payroll department. I never see it, and a lot of work lies behind that. Nobody turns around to me and says, 'Jean, isn't that wonderful, all that you're doing?' " I think training is everything when the training is proper. Dick was helped out a great deal because his mother worked. She didn't mess around, so he was already disposed that way. Training and expectation. People can get very accustomed to expectation from another person, and to the extent that you are willing to yield on your side, that becomes the standard.

At another meeting some of the same thinking is echoed. Kitty as a panel member is asked how much her husband helps out at home. She states she doesn't go along with the women who complain that they have to do most of the work. She speaks with her usual inimitable dry humor, which sends the audience into laughter throughout her comments:

I had the fortune to marry a man who was catered to completely by his mother. He would have died of thirst because he didn't know how to turn on the faucet. Well, he learned. If his socks were dirty, there is no reason why he couldn't put them in the washing machine. We both work. So when he didn't have any clean socks, he figured out what to do. If he came home expecting dinner, I told him he had an expense account. "Have a big lunch that will last you for the day."

At another time, she said, "I take the positive approach. I just don't do things I don't want to do, and they get done by someone else." Nevertheless, she devises schemes and lists to enable everyone, including her husband, to participate. She makes sure that the shopping list is ready and menus planned, that enough money is left for the housekeeper, etc. Both Peter and Kitty agree that when they attempt to discuss who should do what, they tend to get into arguments, more than if they just let things evolve, as they put it.

Sandy recounts for Richard and me the happenings at one meeting where husband participation had come up for discussion. Apparently there were two who were "annoyed as all get-out" at their husbands. They think their husbands don't do anything, while the husbands think they are "the most terrific helpmates," "50 percent everything partners." What Sandy has learned herself, she tells us, is not to do things. She gives an example of how she used to get annoyed when Richard hadn't made one of the two beds that had to be done at the country house and four o'clock on Sunday came around. They would leave around that time. She decided to ignore the unmade bed and not let it bother her. "Sure enough, he made it." Richard does the lawn, takes care of the car, and is involved with "the girls' educational stuff." She has learned how to make requests for things to be done around the house so that Richard hears her and does them. She finds that it is more difficult for her to ask than for him to do things.

Richard responds:

Yes, that's true. I don't think much about that stuff. I wander around too often in my own world, so I don't just see it. If she asks me, I have not much problem doing it. I think most of those women have a level of expectation about what someone ought to do without being asked. I don't have a whole lot of models that say I am to do something like that. I know my father, even though my mother worked—my father just passed through our lives from a development point of view. My mother was supposed to raise the kids. Cooking, my father right up to the point he retired— she used to come home and cook. . . . We had a housekeeper, but that was *her* job. I didn't see anything else.

Earlier Richard said:

I have this philosophy "Them that can does." There are some people in this world who view that time is designed to shove into it as much as you possibly can and others of us who believe time is there to do as little as possible. Sandy is of the former category. She has an enormous capacity to accomplish. She has a generally positive view of the world. She is forward-looking. Those attributes help her do an incredible amount. I am basically lazy. She unfortunately has to expand out to fill the void that I create or nothing gets done. Although she has learned that if she gets abusive, I will probably do something to avoid pain. [Sandy agreed.] It does work to a point. There is a point beyond which she can't push me and then I say I can't do any more and go and sit in a corner and do absolutely nothing.

What Richard is saying is that purposely leaving things undone is obviously a technique adopted by the husband as well as the wife. What is important is the degree to which it is employed. Standards can be lowered, and often are. All the women tell stories about this. If the house isn't spotless, so what? If there are dust balls under the couch, so what? If the housekeeper ruins a piece of clothing, so what? As long as the laundry gets done. And so it goes. If the husband can't tolerate lower standards and refuses to do anything to rectify the situation himself, that may spell trouble. It appears that when the husband goes into a marriage with a successful career woman, he has to accept her as a partner and be willing to be one as well (to varying degrees, to be sure). Otherwise the marriage will not work. The less he participates, the more people have to be hired to pick up the slack. There has to be a back-up system for every contingency; in reality the husband is often part of this back-up system. If the woman finds herself doing everything, she is doing something very wrong, according to the other women. She is not handling her husband or the situation correctly.

These women do not see any sense in being long-suffering, submissive women. I believe that this attitude is an important clue to the workings of their marriages. The traditional marriage supposedly offered the woman financial security. In a sense, the woman was an extension of her husband; her role was to support him in his endeavors and cater to his needs—often to the exclusion of her own—so that he could meet his responsibilities as the sole breadwinner. She looked to have her needs met vicariously through her husband. Baruch, Barnett, and Rivers (1983:58) note that marriage cannot protect a woman from depression, it won't guarantee her a sense of self-esteem, nor will it make her feel in control of her life. Since the women in the success subculture, on the whole, appear to have a definite sense of being in charge of their lives, they do not look to marriage to fulfill such needs. They have their careers and financial independence. Consequently, there is room for actual partnership. Thus, my informants, at least, have emancipated themselves from the traditional dominant-subordinate relationship that Miller (1976), discusses in her book *Toward a New Psychology of Women.*

It is often recognized in the women's discussions at meetings that they do not spend enough time with their husbands, and vice versa, because of their hurried schedules. As one put it, "We have become almost like roommates." There is a consensus that setting aside an evening or some other time when they can interact with each other is essential. The dilemma of finding time can be resolved in many instances by hiring a babysitter. For other couples the problem may be quite complicated, especially if one or both partners travel a lot. Jean, who travels extensively, says that if her business covers days before and after a weekend in another city she makes it a point to come home over the weekend, even if she is as far away as California, and to return to her business in California at the end of the weekend. This is not feasible for everyone, of course. Some couples may actually like more space for themselves. Those who need or want to see each other more may be forced to change jobs.

Finding time to see each other is not often a great problem for my informants. They have their weekend houses and often spend evenings together, although a couple of them are quite child-focused and spend a good deal of time with the children, leaving little for themselves. Neither my informants nor their husbands travel much.

Well, what do the husbands do? Let's take them one by one.

Robert comes home earlier than Anna and spends time with Michael—takes him for a walk or plays with him. He shops for things they are out of, something most New Yorkers do on a daily basis, and picks up the dinner, maybe a chicken or something else to cook. Usually the menu is his choice. The day I spent with Anna, I overheard him calling to say that he was going to pick up pasta and sauce for dinner. She volunteered to pick up the greens for salad. When we got to their apartment, Robert had started the water for the pasta, but she ended up doing the cooking and setting the table with the "help" of Michael. She asked Robert several times to set the table, but he replied facetiously, "I can't, I am being interviewed." He confesses he really likes to cook and used to do it most of the time. But now that Michael has grown, he finds it a nuisance because Michael always wants to participate, and it gets too messy. Robert did clear the table and helped put the dishes in the dishwasher. Later I saw him take the garbage out without being asked. Anna was talking to me at the time. The housekeeper takes care of most other things. They have someone come in to do the heavy cleaning every other week. Recently the housekeeper agreed to cook supper for them on the days Michael goes to nursery school. Robert takes care of their plants. He also does the gardening at their new weekend house. He obviously likes that and was in fact reading a book on gardening when we arrived and continued to look at it now and then throughout the evening. Anna put things out to be taken to the country that weekend, checking with Robert on what she should take as she went along. He didn't participate otherwise. Anna told me that once in an emergency she took Michael to the office in the morning and Robert picked him up there in the afternoon and took him home.

At Kitty and Peter's house, Peter comes home later than she from work, around 7–7:30 P.M. Their breakfast, he says, is one of everybody helping themselves, adding, "If you asked Kitty, she would probably tell you she makes breakfast." Until recently Kitty would prepare a dinner consisting of soup or frozen dinners. Their housekeeper would already have fed Bridgit and bathed her. Their new housekeeper, however, has agreed to cook dinner for them, to Kitty's great relief.

Most of the time I was there, Peter looked after Bridgit, including helping her into her pajamas. Peter says he never cooks. Kitty corrected him, saying, "You're not giving yourself enough credit. He does a lot of barbecuing at the country house since I gave him a fancy barbecue grill." This is another indirect way of delegating. Kitty apparently is a good cook. Before the birth of their first child, they entertained a great deal, and she made elaborate meals. Peter says, "I help out—approaching sharing." Kitty comments: "You really are very good when you're around." Apparently Peter sometimes work late, although he says he has kept pretty regular hours for a long time.

Kitty says that she is the planner and Peter the executor. They do most things together as a family. During Kitty's pregnancy Peter would take Bridgit to the park or to museums on the weekends they spent in New York without being asked because Kitty suffered from "pregnancy sickness." She says that this was the one time she didn't have energy to spare and couldn't wait to be "not pregnant" again.

Peter has stayed home twice in three years to look after Bridgit when Kitty had to go out of town and the housekeeper was sick. They say they discuss this sort of emergency when it arises, and the one whose career will suffer least by absence on the occasion takes the responsibility for Bridgit. Peter has also come home twice from the office to relieve the housekeeper when Kitty's plane was delayed. When she arrived, he returned to the office. Kitty has taken Bridgit to the office on two occasions, and her secretary looked after her while Kitty attended meetings.

In the country Peter takes care of all the repair work on the house. He had finished the repair of the first house they had bought, which became too small when Bridgit was born, and is now doing repair work on their second house. Kitty does not help with this. Peter also states that when things get messy at the weekend house, he does the cleaning, because his threshold for cleanliness is lower than Kitty's. Two college girls come in to clean during the summer.

At Catherine and George's house a clear demarcation of work has been made. Catherine is the one who often comes to the defense of husbands if they are criticized at meetings, saying they compensate by doing other important things such as finance planning. At the weekend house George takes care of contractors and workmen, although he consults her. She says she has a definite input in decision-making. She always does the cooking and George the cleaning up. They don't have a dishwasher in the country as yet. George professes to know only how to fry eggs. To some extent he is of the traditional school and wants to maintain that image, although in reality he does more than one would expect such a man to do. He looks after Steve on the two weekday evenings when Catherine studies, but not on the weekends, when she usually studies in the mornings. Then Catherine takes Steve to a babysitter who has a child his age. George says that when he is looking after Steve he comes home and reads the newspaper while Steve plays, or he takes him for a walk to his older son's house "just for the hell of it." When Steve made a mess in the kitchen while I was at the house, George was the one who cleaned it up. Catherine says he is more involved with Steve now that the child is old enough to respond. George never participated in diapering, etc. when Steve was small.

For that matter, George did not want another child when he and Catherine married, partly because he already had three grown children from his previous marriage and because of his age. When Catherine found herself pregnant, she felt that she couldn't go through an abortion, and she wanted the experience of having a child, although that had not figured in her plans when she remarried.

Catherine has the responsibility for shopping. All staples are bought in the country and taken home. She picks up daily shopping on her way home from work or at her lunch hour. She does not do any housework or laundry. Her housekeeper, who sleeps out, keeps the house clean; another person comes in every other week for the heavy cleaning. There is also a laundress. Catherine says that she will be very happy if she never has to lift a broom again for the rest of her life.

When she is traveling, about six times a year, George takes over. He minimizes what he has to do. The housekeeper is there at 8:30 in the morning, and all he has to do is to put Steve to bed at night. If he wants to go out, he asks the housekeeper to stay. He neglects to mention that his 18-month-old son needs constant supervision. Catherine laughingly tells a story about what she was told when she returned from a trip. Her housekeeper said, "Dont tell Mr. G., but you should see the house in the morning when you're away. Everything strewn about, cereal all over." George, according to Catherine, "doesn't know how to interpret silence. He thinks all is well when there is quiet, not realizing that's the danger point with Steve. He sits there calmly reading his paper."

They often have simple dinners, such as cold cuts, which George likes, and they help themselves. Catherine makes a point, however, of preparing a formal sit-down dinner one night during the week. George is willing to make an omelette for himself when she is not home.

Richard gets up before Sandy and will make breakfast for Elizabeth and "entertain" her while Sandy gets ready. Then he leaves for work. He comes home generally around 7–7:30 P.M. He says he doesn't do much then but "entertain" the family. Sandy says that he often makes a salad while they talk in the kitchen on the days she is home and is cooking. She loves to cook. Richard likes it too, and on weekends meals, including menu-planning, are always a joint undertaking. Richard always cleans up when Sandy cooks, unless his daughters are there. Then they get to do it. He also orders Chinese food, he notes laughingly—"I set out the plates," says Sandy; "and I clean the dishes," counters Richard.

Depending on the situation, either one of them will read Elizabeth a bedtime story. It is easier for them than for many others to go out because they have a sleep-in housekeeper.

In the country Richard does the shopping and runs errands in the morning. He will often do the laundry when necessary. He mows the lawn and takes care of the car.

Karin and Andre have an unusual situation because he is away at school most of the time. When he is home, he participates in everything, including diapering and dressing the children. He also fixes things around the house. He loves to cook and does so when he is at home. When his father-in-law, a gourmet cook, is visiting, he finds himself displaced from the kitchen. Since he is home only every other weekend, much of the child care falls to Karin. The housekeeper is in charge of the children when Karin is away. One of Karin and Andre's problems is that Lise often competes for her mother's attention.

The daily function of the husband in the family, his attitude toward his wife and her career, and his involvement, generally extensive, with the children—seeing these in some detail contributes greatly, of course, to an understanding of how these social systems work. To sum up, the husbands are generally successful in their own right in their own fields, most earning a substantial amount of money. With the possible exception of Robert, they married with the knowledge that their wives were committed to their own careers. No doubt having successful wives, apart from the obvious economic advantages, adds to their status and prestige. They show respect for their wives and acceptance of their careers both in words and in action. Despite relatively traditional backgrounds, they have been willing to learn and to participate in household chores and in child care to varying degrees, perhaps out of sheer self-protection for some. The women simply expect their participation; and I do suspect that their lives would be rather miserable if the husbands didn't acquiesce. Involvement with the children appears to give all the husbands pleasure.

Rapoport and Rapoport (1976) found that husbands of successful career women usually participate to quite an extent in family chores. Some researchers think that the more the careeer woman contributes to the family status and living standards, the more bargaining power she has in obtaining husband participation. Model (1982:194–95) and her associates found in a small subsample of equal-earner couples that one of the effects was that "the smaller the income differential between spouses, the greater male housework participation becomes.

The women do not appear to have thought through why they accept the overall management responsibility for their children and the household, except that it is expected of them. Catherine comments that leaving the main responsibility to the woman seems to be the last vestige of the traditional woman's role to go. Kitty, against her usual advice to leave things undone, says, "Somebody has to fill the void." Sandy, as if just now realizing that she has accepted this role, says with some wonderment, "That's right. Only this morning, I was the one to call the electrician. Why is that? I'll have to talk with Richard about this."

Somehow the women draw a line beyond which they don't push their husbands or expect them to participate. That line is drawn, I believe, where they feel that the husband's resistance outweighs the benefit of his participation, the point of diminishing return, and also the point where they themselves by tradition and training simply do things without questioning why. In an area where they meet resistance, they will try to find a way around it—which is what Kitty did, for example, in getting Peter a barbecue grill. Barbecuing is an activity that is culturally quite acceptable for a male, and Peter has willingly taken on this job. One could call this manipulation on Kitty's part, although Peter is quite aware of her purpose in giving him the grill. Perhaps the acceptance of the overall management of their social system by these strong-willed women is balanced for them by the many things their husbands do do, by the support they give, but most importantly by the women's conscious or unconscious appreciation of the considerable power they have in the relationship, especially in decision-making. There is a delicate balance of power and of give and take in these interdependent relationships.

It may be a different situation if the wife is more successful and earns more money than the husband. In Anna and Robert's case this does not seem to matter; Robert is successful in his field, although he earns less money. Karin and Andre express sensitivity about Karin's supporting his graduate education. The other husbands earn the same or much more than their wives. Should there be any changes in these situations, the potential for difficulties is there. To quote Nadelson and Nadelson (1980:96–97), "It is important to recognize that areas of conflict and dissonance in dual-career couples stem from intrapsychic as well as sociocultural factors. Issues of competition, jealousy, and unrealized expectations or failure to resolve dependency problems from the past play a part in addition to administrative and reality-oriented concerns." It is important also to add that these aspects "are not substantially and qualitatively different from those problems arising in any marital situation."

So, despite the time pressure, the requirement that husbands participate in household chores and child care, the women having the overall management responsibility, and the women's need to use strategies to maximize their husbands' participation, the couples clearly feel that the satisfaction and the benefits they derive from the marriage outweigh any disadvantages. This dovetails with the findings of several other researchers. For example, St. John-Parsons' (1978) study of families that had two careers continuously drew the same conclusions. Nadelson and Nadelson (1980:91–109) discuss the difficulties and the benefits from a psychological and sociocultural point of view. They cite a number of studies to support their view that there can be a positive effect on each member of the dual-career family—on husband, wife, and child. Simpson and England (1982:147–71) found "that marital interaction is enhanced when both spouses are employed."

Less affluent families, obviously, cannot afford as many support systems as the families in the success subculture. Bernard wrote in her 1982 update of *The Future of Marriage:* "One result for wives [who are employed], found almost everywhere in the industrialized world (Bernard, 1979), has been overload, for the sharing of the provider role by wives has not always meant the sharing of household or child-care roles by husbands" (1982:299). Even though husbands are an area of complaint, the women in the success subculture clearly are in relatively egalitarian marriages and also are in a position to hire support systems that minimize whatever lack of husband participation there may be. The costs are still there, but the benefits prevail.

4

Financial Arrangements

"Financial arrangements certainly tell you a lot about a marriage, don't they?" comments Sandy in response to a question. In my informants' marriages, the financial arrangements reflect the partners' autonomy as well as their interdependence. They vary from couple to couple.

When they married, Catherine and George sat down and added up their expenses and divided everything down the middle. They pay their assigned bills monthly. Now and then they recheck to make certain that the amounts are approximately equal. They find this the least complicated method because George has additional expenses related to his ex-wife and the children from his first marriage. The couple's assets are also separate. The co-op was Catherine's before they married and still is. George had bought a country house just before they married, and that is his. He also pays the considerable restoration expenses on the house. They have separate credit cards, and they file separate income tax returns.

Robert and Anna put their paychecks into their joint checking account. She earns more than Robert. She says that this has never been an issue with them—"we spend all the money anyway as fast as it comes in." They do have separate savings accounts. She balances the checking account "because I am the financial person in the family; besides, each time Robert comes near it, it takes weeks to straighten it out." In short, Anna is in charge of the financial management and planning for the family. She prepares everything for the accountant who does their joint tax return. Their co-op and country house are owned jointly. They have a joint credit card, in her name, because she uses it for business. Each has separate charge cards.

According to Kitty, her income fluctuates heavily with the market. Sometimes she earns as much as 50 percent more than Peter; at other times her income is equal to his or lower. It evens out in the long run, she says. They have separate bank accounts and credit cards. Here is her summary of their arrangements:

We have a joint resource management account plus cash. We operate pretty separately for having been married this long [seven years]. I pay for the house in the country and the housekeeper out of my income. Peter pays for the apartment in New York, which is in his name. The house is in mine. He pays the utilities. This just evolved; [we] never sat down and discussed it. It certainly worked out conveniently. . . . [Kitty is talking in her usual facetious way.] I hate paying bills . . . so he took that over. We have never balanced our accounts in all the years we have been married. I just hope the bank has a good accountant who catches mistakes. I just can't be bothered, and I'm the financial person too. Another thing I refuse to have anything to do with is income tax. I make him do that too. . . . It depresses me so much, so I refuse to do anything but sign the return. Naturally, he feels I'm not giving him credit for all the nuisance of paying bills and doing the income tax return. . . . I am the one who wants to sit down and do some long-term financial planning, long-term life planning. Peter is more willing to let things evolve. Within the context of a very vague plan, things sort of happen, like the decision to buy the house, the co-op. I felt that was part of a long-term plan to start establishing ourselves.

Karin and Andre have a joint checking account. She confesses that, since the birth of her first child, she hasn't bothered balancing the account. They do keep, however, some approximate track of what they have, so as not to overdraw. Complications can develop because they live most of the time in two different cities. In the past she always balanced her checking account, and it used to bother her no end if it didn't balance. Here is an example of trading off something which was important in the past for what she now considers more pressing or more important use of her time. Theirs is at present a one-income family; it is her paycheck that goes into the account.

Andre is concerned that Karin does very little personal shopping. He would like for her to buy some more clothes, but she says she doesn't have time. What they buy is usually for the family, and they do that shopping together. They don't use credit cards. She has one in her name which she got when she returned to New York. They have separate charge cards. Karin owns a house in her native country, where they will spend their next vacation. Most of the execution of plans must of necessity be done by Karin, because she is here and Andre is not. She is the one who looks for the other apartment they will need when their sublet is up at the end of the summer. He will look at the ones she picks as possibilities. Karin emphasizes that they discuss all their planning together, however loose that planning is. She notes that she gets very annoyed when people make insensitive references to her supporting her husband through school. Andre too apparently has a good deal of feeling about this. He talks about how everybody takes it for granted that he will look for a job in New York City because Karin is working here. No one realizes that he has built up a network of contacts in the city where he is studying and where he acted as consultant in his field. The guests at their house when I was present all (including myself) went on the assumption that he would give up his opportunities elsewhere and settle in New York. It is a reversal, it seems, of the traditional thinking that the wife should give up her ambitions to follow her husband. No one except Karin and Andre seemed to recognize that compromises will have to be worked out. They have an ongoing dialogue about opportunities and possibilities.

Sandy tells her story:

How we handle ours [financial arrangements] is relatively simple. It's yours, mine, and ours. That reflects how we came together. It's more complicated now, because more things are falling into "ours." On a transaction basis, I handle all the bill-paying and spending. . . . Richard writes out his checks to doctors, ex-wife, the kids, schools, camps. . . . He pays for the car and a lot of the restaurant stuff and vacations. He often pays more or a higher percentage of that than I do.

It evolved when we first moved in together and created a joint checking account. I said, "This is wonderful, you are going to balance this every month, because I really hate that job, and you are going to write all the bills." But it turns out he has no tolerance for spending money. It sends him into a nosedive . . . . It doesn't faze me in the least [to spend money]. If he goes [and] dips his card in the bank computer and sees a negative balance, he thinks we are in debt. I think it's just something he doesn't have to worry about.

Sandy goes on to say that when they do their regular yearly "asset value look" at themselves, if it should turn out that one is gaining and the other losing financially, that wouldn't sit well at all. They now have so many accounts in the children's and their own names that they need to do some financial planning this year. "We really have money in every possible bucket."

Richard writes Sandy a check twice monthly for the joint account. She puts most of her paycheck into the joint account, unless she decides to put something in investment. They don't make an effort to put in exactly the same amount. Over the year there may be a thousand dollars' difference.

Sandy points out that they have very different attitudes toward money. "Richard is viewing everything, 'Suppose we all lost our jobs tomorrow. . . .' I don't think that is going to happen, so I'm not going to worry about it. He worries enough for the both of us anyway."

They have separate credit cards. Neither one of them wants the other's business expenses on their bills. Sandy remarks, "You can always tell when you open the bills, whose it is. His is zero, mine is several hundred dollars."

Sandy views the house in the city and the house in the country as investments, while Richard apparently sees them more as shelter and recreation. He has always kept his money "in 5 percent savings accounts." Now, according to Sandy, "he has gotten up to a money market investment account, but he doesn't put money in it unless he is absolutely sure he's not withdrawing for eight months." Richard has stopped watching Sandy balancing the checkbook, because it made him "frenzied" when he saw her put parentheses around balances. To Sandy, as she said, this is simply good cash management. She deposits money to cover the deficit the next day. "Now his job when I am paying the bills is to put the stamps on the envelopes. It sounds silly, but then I won't resent the fact that he is sitting there watching TV. That's fine."

My informants' financial arrangements are not of the old traditional kind, where property, accounts, and credit cards mostly were in the husband's name. The women are autonomous and partners with their husbands, and vice versa. In most instances, they share about equally in expenses. Each couple has worked out a system with which they are comfortable. Three of the women use their maiden names, and I don't think it would sit well with any one of them to have accounts or credit cards in any other name.

In the area of financial arrangements, one might expect that my informants would be more forceful in delegating the bookkeeping to their partners or would simply refuse to do it, as Kitty has. Catherine's case is different from the others, because each partner takes care of his/her own and the assigned household bills only. The others have the major responsibility for bookkeeping and financial management. The reasons for this are probably varied. One might speculate that by accepting this role, whether by design or not, they are more in control of family decisions. This does not seem of much significance in Kitty's situation. Despite Peter's handling of the bookkeeping, Kitty appears to have at least an equal part in actual planning and decision-making. Sandy clearly is willing to pay the price of doing the bookkeeping because it enables her to live the kind of family life she wants, namely, not to worry about money. Realistically, according to her, there is no reason to worry. She is in charge. Both Karin and Anna seem to have the main role in decision-making, since they determine whether the family can afford something or not. They are also the ones who have to implement the financial decisions that they and their partners make. For example, Anna handled all the financial arrangements when buying their country house. (I learned this from her secretary, who made some of the calls.)

In Catherine's case the delineation of control is most clear-cut. She and George have to consult each other about any family decision that involves money, to determine how it can be financed. Each has a veto power over something he or she doesn't want.

The financial arrangements, then, even though three of my informants carry the major responsibility for them, work as support systems too. Their combined incomes constitute a large amount of money that they have at their disposal. It is used for the benefit of both partners and for the children, but the women have considerable power in determining how the money shall be spent on both discretionary and nondiscretionary items in every sphere of their social systems. However, they appear to do this with their partners' feelings in mind when making decisions that affect their husbands or the family as a whole. How much weight these feelings are given differs in each situation and for each couple.

It seems clear that my informants' equal contribution toward their family's expenses and high living standards have a bearing on their husbands' considerable participation in child care and household responsibilities, as Model (1982:195) and her colleagues found in their small subsample of equal earners. Their income and prestige, undoubtedly, have a pervasive effect on their husbands' attitude toward them in every area. There is little room for playing the traditional roles in these families. The husbands see their wives as partners and equals.

5

Maternity and the Child

The care of their children is the one area where women in
the success subculture allow themselves to express some
concern, directly or indirectly. The topics and discussions
in the Working Mothers' group lead me to believe that they
need affirmation that they are doing the right thing by their
children. They obviously want them to be happy and are
not immune to implied criticism from "nonworking" mothers and others. They apparently feel vulnerable, and sometimes express their irritation in counterattacks.

Since we are in a transition period when the mothers of
young children are moving into the labor market in increasing numbers, the reality is that for better or for worse, the
children will have to adjust to the mothers' work patterns.
Society's assumption is still that the responsibility for child
rearing rests with the mother, the husband being an aux-
iliary.

Some questioning of this attitude can be discerned in the
media. For example, David Wessel (1984), in an article, one
of a series, in the *Wall Street Journal*, speaks to the plight of
the working father: "Today's ideal middle-class father is
supposed to change diapers, do housework, be emotionally
involved with his children—without shirking his duties at
work." He reports that paternity leave is available in 119
large corporations but is seldom utilized. Only 8 companies

say that men have taken advantage of it. The fact is, as one man notes, that one is not really expected to take the time. Working fathers seem to be experiencing something similar to what faces career women, who often take only a fraction of their maternity leave for fear that their seriousness about their careers will be questioned. Apparently the men do not take paternity leaves for the same reason. In another article about "The Working Mother as Role Model" in *The New York Times Magazine*, Anita Shreve (1984) discusses several mental health professionals' study findings and their thinking about two-career parents. She describes as an example one egalitarian couple who seem genuinely to share in the care of their children. She also reports on "an intriguing study" of 17 role-reversed families in which the husband stays home full time and is the primary parent while the mother works full time. Experimentation is taking place, and obviously warrants media attention.

When years have passed and the children of the baby-boom generation have become grown-ups themselves, psychological theories no doubt will have been revised to reflect new norms in child development. At present, there are still murky waters to swim through. Is it good or bad to leave your child and go to work? It depends largely on whom you listen to. All too often one can hear mothers who need to justify their working say, "I have to for financial reasons." Others who work because they want to are left with feelings of guilt they cannot easily rationalize. They simply have to live with them until society as a whole becomes more accepting of working mothers.

Successful career women who are also mothers do not work for financial reasons alone, although the money they earn is essential to their lifestyles. They work because they possess the personality characteristics described in earlier chapters. They are autonomous and intelligent; they like power and want to be in control of their lives. They obtain prestige, recognition, and money from their work. They are energized by their success.

The upbringing of the child is in a way an unknown to them, something not entirely predictable or within their control. They cannot completely master the development of children as they think they can their jobs. The rules are unclear, so the outcome is uncertain. They can only do their best within the framework of their own social systems. These observations dovetail with the findings of Baruch, Barnett, and Rivers (1983:80–81), who found that motherhood is one of the main sources of distress for women because of the unpredictability of their children's development. When there is conflict, mothers tend to be blamed, or they blame themselves. Their sense of well-being is lowered.

Caplan and Hall-McCorquodale (1985) in a study on "Mother Blaming in Major Clinical Journals" found that mental health professionals tend to place all too much blame on mothers. Even though many more women are working, and parenting is shared more in two-parent families, the mother is still held responsible for the child's problems and is often the only source of information about them (1985:352). The mother-child relationship, certainly, is important, but many other factors have significant impact on the child's development. In clinical writings fathers are not "blamed" for their absence or lack of involvement. Very few professionals hold the system responsible which leaves the burden of child rearing entirely on the mother. Chess, Thomas, and Birch (1965), on the basis of a ten-year longitudinal study, pointed out in their book *Your Child Is a Person* how much unjustified guilt this total responsibility leaves with mothers. Chess and Thomas (1982) and others have advocated for years the shifting of emphasis from who is doing the child rearing to the child's need for nurturing and caring.

The traditional mothers of the not-too-distant past had books and theories to guide them, granted not always very successful ones and frequently creating guilt if not followed.

These books and theories, however, often condemn the way today's women handle their children, the early separation and so on. Fraiberg (1977), for example, strongly suggests that mothers stay home with their children through the early formative years. Since women are now sharing the experience of going to work with millions of other women, they are no longer exceptions.

Yet the uncertainty makes women who want undisputed control of their lives feel vulnerable. It is the "I" versus the sustaining crowd all over again. If they accept that their success cannot be accomplished alone, there need not be so much worry. They certainly use their sustaining crowd to help them care for their children the best way they can. In fact, they are in a position financially to provide good, steady caretakers; the less affluent may not be able to do as well. The latter women have to devise schemes for child care that are more complicated and less foolproof to enable them to go to work.

The following remarks, made at a Working Mothers' luncheon, reflect their reactions to and concerns about how the world views them as mothers.

A woman who lives in the suburbs and works in the city said,

You are an anomaly when you work. Especially in church. Women just don't work. I sometimes don't even tell people I work. But people are very nice. My daughter's friends' parents transport her around everywhere.

Another woman responded:

I find my friends are not very nice about it, sort of hostile. Maybe they are feeling guilty because they are not working. I don't care what they do, but they really seem to care about what I do.

Someone else said,

I find it's not a good idea to get into discussions about the fact that you work and they don't. I have heard so many times from really close friends of mine, "You have to do what is right for you." Like, you have your morals, I have mine. I can't conduct that kind of conversation and feel I have won.

Another noted that people asked her, "How can you leave your children at such an early age?"

Like they are saying, how can you be such a horrible mother and go into the city and leave your children and let someone else raise them? It used to bother me with my first daughter. I used to get very upset about it.

Someone interjected, "and you know they are out on the tennis court. They are not with that two-year-old." The other continued her story:

Quantity versus quality. I used to say that a lot, but I wasn't sure whether it was real. After being home for five weeks when I had my second daughter, I really know that's true. I was horrible when I was with her all the time. I had no patience, I was tired. I have much more time for her now, because my time is better planned and I don't feel I have to do everything around the house anymore. So I really don't let it bother me anymore.

Someone added,

There is a lot of pressure on women who are staying home to be in the office. I think that a lot of the hostility is not really directed toward you, but toward the media that's making them feel guilty for staying home. You know, they should be superwomen and do everything.

Many agreed that in the suburbs working women are ostracized and not on the same wave length as the traditional women. One woman, who, after being a housewife for ten years, was divorced and had to go to work to support herself and the children, found that all her friends cheered her on. "Atta girl, Carol, go to it." They knew that in her circumstances they would have to do the same thing. Apparently they could identify with her and enjoy her success. She conceded that her working was acceptable because it wasn't voluntary.

I have heard similar discussions at other luncheons. The same kind of attitude is encountered by the women who live in the city when, for example, they go for some occasion to their child's nursery school. They feel the teachers treat them differently from the other mothers. "Look who's here. Isn't this a treat? Aren't you dressed beautifully?" mimicked Louise, "and I was in my most defunct business clothes." Someone else reported that the hostility of the other mothers was pretty heavy when she arrived at her child's nursery school. She was not included in their conversation. It worried her because she would like her child to have friends in school. Betsy told her not to worry. She had had a similar experience, and her daughter won out. She made friends, and the other children demanded that Carla come visit with them. "There is hardly a day now that she hasn't a date."

Apparently the traditional mothers also have a problem in dealing with the housekeepers when they bring the children over. They don't want to be friends with the housekeepers. Betsy had handled this situation by telling the mothers that she doubted that her housekeeper wanted to be friends with them. She herself would not want their housekeepers as friends. If her housekeeper takes Carla to their house and it's far away, she can look after the children and the mother can go take a nap if she wants to. "That works like a charm every time." Others expressed concern that their children were not invited to birthday parties when the mothers were not around to pick them up at school. When Eve was home on maternity leave, she found that her daughter was frequently invited to such parties, but the invitations petered out when she returned to work.

At the playground the housekeepers congregate in one area and the mothers in another, so that the two sets of children do not play together. This does not seem to bother the career women. They think the caste system is rather amusing; it becomes a concern only when their children enter regular nursery school. Then the career women spend a good deal of time on the telephone arranging their children's social calendars, because they do not see the other children's mothers or housekeepers at school or in the park. Some of the career women express a distaste for sitting on a park bench, as they have done on their brief maternity leaves. They find it boring. Catherine mentioned that she thought there was something to be said for the park bench, "But you don't have to spend eight hours a day doing it. You can learn a lot from other women that way and compare notes." She tries to get together with other mothers at work as a substitute for the park. This kind of function is, of course, also served by the Working Mothers' group. Catherine commented on this also:

I always take away with me a practical hint, like getting two contacts for Steve's pre-nursery and nursery school. It is reassuring to hear others reaffirm my own convictions re food for example. I don't worry too much about eating habits if he is strong and healthy. He can do without vegetables and rice if he refuses. I don't want any battles over that, and that's what the others said at lunch.

Sandy noted:

Catherine doesn't really know how to be a mother. She has had no experience with children. She is learning it step by step and she needs reaffirmation. That's what the Working Mothers' group is all about.

On the whole my informants express very little overt guilt about their upbringing of their children. "I'm trying to do the best I can and that's all I can do," they seem to be saying. They work hard at being good mothers.

As with everything else, experience helps. Jean in the pilot study is talking about new mothers:

They don't yet understand years of service with children. They are still tighter [uptight]. I recall when my daughter was born. I had a neighbor who encouraged me to return to work. Someone at work said, "You're going to miss your child's first step." I ran home that night and called my neighbor, saying, "I just realized I'm going to miss my child's first step." She looked at me: "You nitty, don't you understand that the child's first step is the first step you see? If you are standing at the stove, turning the spaghetti around, and the kid takes a step when you turn around, that's the first step. What difference does it make?" I said, "Oh, you've got a point there." But that's having someone straightening you out all the time, and you need that.

Epstein (1981:370) discusses an interesting point regarding guilt and ambivalence about child care arrangements. She thinks the busy woman lawyer and mother is insulated from the sanctions of the world around her because she doesn't have the time for casual conversation, popular magazines, and television, where she would be exposed to critical evaluation. Thus, the more she works, the less guilt she experiences. The one who has disapproving relatives and friends is more apt to be ambivalent about her mothering role and consequently experiences more guilt.

According to Kagan (1983), it is not only the traditional housewife and mother who disapproves of the working mother. Working Americans per se, including many working mothers, think it is bad for children under 6 years of age to have working mothers. She writes:

The ambivalent, even critical, attitude of many American workers toward working mothers is one of the most unsettling findings to come out of the survey of the American workplace carried out last summer by the Public Agenda Foundation, a nonprofit research organization headed by Daniel Yankelovich. (Kagan 1983:18)

Whether or not a mother has to work for financial reasons apparently does not make much difference. More than half of working Americans in this survey do not approve of mothers working.

Kagan also says that

The majority of American workers believes—over a quarter, strongly—that a woman who wants to work instead of staying home and raising children should not have them in the first place. Here again, men and women are split significantly (56 to 43 percent) on whether work-oriented women also should be mothers. (1983:20)

Kagan's opening statement seems all too correct:

When a society changes faster than the ideas of people living in it, the pioneers on the cutting edge of those changes rarely have an easy time. (1983:18)

Researchers are trying to bring some objectivity into the arena of emotional opinions about working mothers and what effect their working has on their children. Studies are fast emerging. The findings are, interestingly enough, reassuring for the working mothers. Yet more extensive, longitudinal studies are probably needed to convince a rather hostile world.

The findings of one such study, the Family Styles Project, certainly should be encouraging to career women everywhere. Zimmerman and Bernstein (1983) followed 200 mothers, between the ages of 18 and 35, assessing their children at 1, 3, and 6 years of age. The study was carefully controlled and the population studied is thought to be representative of the U.S. white population as a whole. They concluded:

In summary, when the work patterns of 200 mothers were compared to a variety of measures of their children's social, emotional and cognitive development, there was no evidence of negative effects traceable to maternal absence due to their employment. When the maternal ability level [based on intelligence level of the mother] was controlled, children of working mothers tended to do slightly better on cognitive measures, to show no defects in attachment to their mother, to perceive the mothers as equally supportive and to have less traditional sex role perceptions. (1983:424)

Many of the studies described in the literature find that children who have working mothers and fathers who participate in child care and household tasks have less stereotypical sex role perceptions. Other typical findings are that working mothers provide a largely positive role model for their children, that is, if they like their work; the children tend to have a higher evaluation of female competence and to be more independent (Carlson 1982; Johnson and Johnson 1980; Nadelson and Nadelson 1980).

According to Shreve (1984), Dr. Kyle Pruett, associate professor of psychiatry at Yale, found in his four-year study of role-reversed families that the young children in these families were more socially active, more curious, and performed better on adaptive-skill tests than babies in traditional families where the father worked and the mother stayed home. He "believes that one explanation for these positive attributes" is having two "stimulating" parents. The fathers here, the primary parent, jostle, bounce, and tease their children more than mothers, who are more gentle. The mothers, the "coming and going" parent, stimulate their babies' curiosity. On the whole, an increase in interaction between fathers and their children seems to have a positive effect on both father and child that may augur well for the future. Needless to say, these benefits have a positive effect on the working mother as well (Johnson and Johnson 1980; Nadelson and Nadelson 1980).

Most of the women, including those in the pilot study, had uneventful pregnancies and worked literally up to the day their babies were born. The exceptions are Anna and Karin. Anna had to take a prolonged leave to prevent another miscarriage; and Karin had to follow her organization's regulations, which require maternity leave starting three weeks before the due date. Actually, Sandy could be said to have had complications—fibroids—but characteristically she didn't speak of it.

The women tell some funny and some not-so-funny stories about their pregnancies and the way people at work reacted. The pregnancies, they say, did not affect the way they functioned at work at all. They did all the usual things, including travel into the last months. Catherine went on a business trip to the West Coast three weeks before her due date.

Sandy had been put on a project by her "protective" female boss against her wishes when she learned that Sandy was pregnant. The project involved a good deal of taxi transportation between offices. She laughingly tells of how she waved away a male colleague's gallant attempts to assist her out of cabs in the beginning of her pregnancy. Toward the end, she had become immense. There was no longer any waving him off. "Here, take my briefcase, take my hand, heave!"

Jean (pilot study) tells of a first pregnancy lasting into the third week of her tenth month. That week she was in Chicago, being walked up and down the airport by her boss. He believed strongly that walking would bring on delivery. It didn't work. The second time around, Jean was working for a different company and in a senior executive position. This time she went to Boston for a large company meeting, lasting a few days, again past her due date. Unbeknownst to her, the chairman of the firm had a "limo" following the bus that transported members between places, in case she needed to be rushed to a hospital. Everything becomes a lot easier when you are up there and doing very well. The chairman seems to be very much a part of her sustaining crowd.

Jean also tells of the difficulties she experienced at work during her first pregnancy. She had been on a new job only six months when she became pregnant—an unplanned pregnancy. She was the very first woman in her echelon. "My becoming pregnant was an astonishing blow to people at work," she recalled. Part of her job involved addressing groups. "They were still digesting the fact that a very young woman was before them, telling them how to do things. That was a risk for my boss in hiring me in the first place—young, inexperienced and, number three, something to look at."

Her boss had such difficulty dealing with her pregnancy that eventually she was transferred by his superior to someone else who had no problem with it. "Apparently," Jean continues,

he had in his mind, with reason, which is a problem for women, to believe I was leaving. Never asked. Presumably selected me over others. He had taken a risk with me, the first woman in this role. Already he felt he was putting before men something that was awkward and different and might not go down their throats and now she is a pregnant woman, and he is not happy about that. That's on a logical level. On the emotional level, it threw him; he was startled, felt betrayed. He didn't expect it. No one else would have doubted my sincerity and didn't. [If I had it to do over,] instead of saying, "John, I'm pregnant," I would have written him a memo saying: I will take vacation time, I am having a baby etc., etc. I will be returning to work on such and such a date, excluding unforeseen events." Or be so responsive to another person [that] rather than leave questions to be answered, answer them before they were asked. I don't think women do that. It would have been to my advantage. You learn.

Many corporations allow women a six-month maternity leave without pay and an assured position, comparable to the one held, when they return. Companies that provide disability benefits to their employees are required by law to give these benefits to pregnant women (Adams and Winston 1980). How long they stay out with pay after the birth of the child depends on their doctors, who specify the time they think the patient needs to stay home for health reasons.

Catherine relates that she told her boss about her pregnancy when she was more than four months' pregnant. She had squeezed into her old clothes until then. "He was," she said, a bit surprised but basically happy for me. He was mainly concerned with how much time I was taking off and if I was coming back. I told him what I wanted to do, provided it was a healthy baby. I did a little work at home. I did the routine part of the work, but not the original research stuff.

Catherine had an "easy pregnancy" and was in excellent health throughout. She worked until the day before Steve was born. Her doctor signed for eight weeks' disability. She had been in the firm for five years and had never been sick, and so she took two more weeks' vacation time. She could have stayed out longer, "but you lose your exposure, lose your credibility as a serious professional, so in reality you wouldn't want to do that." Because Steve was bottle fed, she didn't have to worry about feedings.

Anna had a "perfect pregnancy" up until six months, when she suddenly had a premature delivery. The baby lived a few hours. After that there were many complications; for three months she was frequently ill, although she went back to work. The following spring she became pregnant again. After fourteen weeks and some surgery, the doctor recommended that she stay home. Although she didn't have to stay in bed, she had to be extremely careful. She had accumulated a lot of sick leave over the years because she had never been sick. With the miscarriage and subsequent complications, she used up much of the sick leave, and soon it ran out. So she was home without pay. When Michael was born, she took six months' maternity leave without pay. She breast-fed Michael for five months and then weaned him before going back to work. She was given a comparable position to the one she had when she left. (The division she had worked in folded after she left.) She moved from one area to another until she got to the division she is presently heading.

Kitty had planned to go back to work six weeks after Bridgit was born, intending to go in four hours a day for two months and to breast-feed the baby at home. As it

turned out, she returned after three weeks, to her colleagues' surprise, saying "I was bored out of my mind."
After two months she worked six hours daily, cutting out
one feeding. She managed this by pumping the milk at the
office and refrigerating it for the next day's feeding. Tech-
nically this meant she was working full time because she
also worked at home. She comments on the difficulties involved in the distance between office and home, having to
rely on subways. Apparently it was rough, but she plans
to try doing the same thing with the new baby. This time
she will take her four weeks' vacation, not maternity leave,
spending it at their country house. Peter will spend two
weeks there after the birth of the baby and then take four-
day weekends for the next two weeks. Their new housekeeper has agreed to stay there five days a week. She has
a 5-year-old child who can play with Bridgit and go to the
beach with them. Kitty is pleased with this arrangement. It
will mean she will be free to do some work if need be. Kitty
describes as the highlight of her day after Bridgit was born
sitting down with material the office sent her daily and with
the *Wall Street Journal.*

Sandy, as noted earlier, had been groomed for a big promotion when she realized she was pregnant and was put
into a staff position instead. Nancy, her friend, was the one
who suggested that Sandy might be pregnant. She herself
couldn't quite believe it. The doctors she consulted varied
in estimated due date because she had fibroids and seemed
much further along than she actually was. This was a com-
plication for which she later had to have surgery. She had
separated from her husband and found another co-op in
her eight month, because he had bought a co-op in the same
house. The fibroids also made her become very large. She
was working on her MBA in the evenings. She worked until
the last day, not knowing it was that. On Christmas Day
she went to her mother's but felt so bad she returned home.
When she finally realized she was in labor, her friend Nancy

went with her to the hospital. After Elizabeth's birth Sandy stayed with her mother for two weeks. She had not yet lined up a housekeeper when she returned home. She breast-fed Elizabeth for four weeks, weaning her in time to return to work. She took six weeks off altogether after scouting around and finding this the norm for women at her professional level. One week before she went back to work, she hired as housekeeper a young woman in the neighborhood. The new housekeeper's mother lived nearby, so that Sandy felt doubly safe, having the mother as back-up. Until then Sandy had taken care of everything herself. She did no work for the office during this time.

After Sandy and Richard's son is born this summer—by Cesarean section, for medical reasons—Sandy will spend some time at the country house until Elizabeth has to return to the city for school, about three weeks. Richard will take two weeks' vacation. They will have a woman there for one week because "Richard is scared of taking care of the baby." If need be, they will keep the woman another week, but Sandy doesn't think it will be necessary.

Karin's organization mandates three months' maternity leave, including the three weeks before the birth. After almost a year in her position in the Far East, Karin became pregnant by plan. The climate was very bad for her. When the baby was due, she went on maternity leave to her native country for three months, then returned to her post. She had a nurse for the baby and breast-fed Lise for five months, going home for feedings. Andre left Asia to go to school when Lise was three months old. Karin finally left three months later, after about two years in her post, because of respiratory difficulties due to the climate. She went on a regular six months' leave and stayed with Andre, who was going to school in the city in which his family lives. While on leave, Karin became pregnant with Marcel. She thinks it was nice of her organization to arrange this leave, although apparently she was entitled to it. She kept her seniority.

She returned to work in New York when she was three to four months' pregnant. She had come to New York beforehand to arrange for an apartment and a housekeeper, both of which she found through a network of friends. Andre remained to finish his education and joined his family every other weekend. One of her parents, who are in their seventies, alternated in staying with her continuously to help out. When Marcel was born, she breast-fed him and continued to do so for about four weeks after she returned to work, skipping one feeding but extracting milk at work and refrigerating it.

The sense one gets is that my informants did what they felt was acceptable for their career positions, except for Anna, who felt that she was gambling with her career. The others allotted themselves the time they thought their companies and/or clients would accept and still view them as serious career women. In short, they would not have stayed out longer even if they could have and wanted to, for fear their reputation as hardworking, conscientious career women would be damaged. They all state that the time taken was sufficient. Some of the other pilot study women even felt that the next time around, they would take less time off, as Kitty decided midway through her maternity leave. For some, perhaps, returning to work is a buffer against stress, as Baruch, Barnett, and Rivers (1983:145) found. When at work, the women do not have to be available to their children at all times, nor do they feel they have to do everything. Unquestionably, there is more structure when one is at work; more control. One can compartmentalize better. One can move from one thing to another in a more orderly fashion when there isn't a child or a household crying for one's attention. At home one might miss the stimulation of work and the rewards derived from it. Besides, there is a physical tiredness and a dimunition of energy as a result of the delivery, which, as discussed earlier, is distressing in itself to the successful career women.

From the career women's point of view, there is another dimension to being at home for an extended period of time, especially for those who are strongly career focused. Most say that they cannot do their office work well at home, and they cannot keep a finger in the pie. For many, keeping up with happenings is vital to the successful performance of their jobs. Kitty, for example, says that in her experience it is difficult to work at home. She does a lot of writing and had thought she could easily do this there, but no matter how she tried and regardless of how many people there were around, she found that the baby wound up with her. This was probably one of the reasons for cutting her maternity leave short. She was not able to devote enough time to her work, and that, I believe, would be stressful to some of the successful career women. Sandy, I was told by her secretary, would call the office every day to check on how things were going when she was away for more than a few days. It clearly is important to her and her career to be certain that her department is functioning well.

Karin, Kitty, and Sandy had always included children in their plans for their lives. Anna was initially ambivalent but decided in the affirmative one day when she was 29 years old. Catherine, as noted, had not figured on a child and became pregnant accidentally. "You feel differently emotionally, once you are [pregnant]," she said, "than you do when you think about a decision rationally in advance." Kitty and Sandy each had their first child when they were around 29 to 30 years of age. Sandy had wanted a child long before. She became pregnant more or less accidentally when her first marriage was on the rocks. Anna was 31 years old, and Catherine and Karin were about 35 when they had their first child. Karin and Kitty have two children, and Sandy will have two children by the end of the summer.

All these children are being cared for by housekeepers during the day. Before they went to prenursery, nursery, and kindergarten programs, they were taken to the park by the housekeepers, or they would visit back and forth with friends. They still do on non-school days.

When Bridgit was six months old, Kitty took the initiative in telephoning neighborhood women who had children Bridgit's age and arranging for four or five of them to get together every day. Her housekeeper met the other house-keepers in the park, and they alternated apartment visits when the weather was bad. The mothers got together once monthly. Kitty says that the housekeepers have become fast friends and get together on their days off, even spend holidays together. One of the housekeepers is Anglo-Saxon and the others are West Indians, an unusual combination to become friends, according to Kitty. This arrangement is an example of the kind of ingenuity the women use in net-working and establishing support systems for their children as well as for themselves.

During the work week Bridgit has breakfast with her parents; then she is taken to nursery school and picked up by the housekeeper. When Kitty comes home around 5:30–5:45 P.M., Bridgit and she usually have a semiplanned project, like making cookies. The day I visited, they had decorated the wastepaper baskets. Before Kitty comes home, Bridgit is bathed by the housekeeper. Formerly the child had dinner with the housekeeper. Now the new housekeeper bathes her and then cooks for the family so that they can have dinner together. Kitty and Peter say that Bridgit has adjusted to their bedtime and stays up with them. Consequently she sleeps relatively late in the morning. She goes with them everywhere, including restaurants if they have dinner out. Their friends all have children, and when they visit each other, the children come along—mostly on Sunday brunches when they are in the city. Their house is clearly child focused. Kitty has remarked a couple of times that it may be too much so. Kitty and Peter have little time for each other with this arrangement.

When they are in the city, they go to museums on the weekends. Recently Bridgit went with them to an auction. She is now a pretty 3-year-old, extremely active and talkative. She likes attention and played with her father a great deal when I was there. He says, "She is becoming more of a professional attention-getter every day." Kitty remarks, "Bridgit is my number one priority, number two is my job, and third is Peter." She laughingly apologizes to Peter. "Sorry, Peter, you come in third."

Anna had arranged for a young woman from her native country to come to the United States as a housekeeper when Michael was born. She remained with them for four months. It didn't work out. "It was like having two babies to take care of." Anna then got Mary through the recommendation of a friend. Mary is an Irish baby nurse and nursemaid. She is still with them. She has had many years' experience with children. She has a fairly strict code as to what is proper for her to do. When Michael starts regular nursery school (private) this fall, Anna is thinking of perhaps getting a more regular housekeeper. She is obviously not keen on this change because Michael loves Mary, they trust her, and they are all quite used to each other by now. She will probably wait until Michael starts kindergarten to make the change.

Michael is a handsome boy with a mischievous smile. He is 3½ years old. He is very bright. Mary shows me how he has written his name. "He likes to be the center of attention and he is," notes Mary. "He is the prince of the parlor. When his mother comes home, he likes to have her complete attention. I can understand that." He gets his father's too, but the father is sometimes tired, according to Mary. She and Michael go to the park all the time, says Mary. Or, when the weather is threatening, they go to some local gardens in the neighborhood that are open to the public. They go in the morning and the afternoon on off-school days. Michael visits with the children of his parents' friends and with some others that he has met at school. He has friends he plays with regularly in the park. Anna believes strongly in making a conscious attempt to find friends who have children Michael's age.

Michael started going to a play program when he was 1½ years old for two hours twice a week. At age 3 he started prenursery school. On one of my visits, Michael tells me what prenursery school he goes to. He also attends a music program across the street for an hour. Mary shows me some songs he has learned, the notes for running, skipping, etc. As she is showing me the notes, Michael tells me what the notes stand for, remembering some Mary has forgotten, and sings a couple of songs for us. Mary says that she has participated in this program. Michael got a very good report card for last year's participation. Anna had told me before that Robert, who is in the field of education, was furious at his child's being rated at this early age.

Mary usually gives Michael dinner and a bath before she leaves in the evening at six; she eats dinner with him. Robert generally does the dinner shopping for Anna and himself, and the time he arrives home therefore varies. He comes home quite early in the summertime, sometimes as early as two o'clock. Mary and Michael are not always home then.

When I arrived at their house the day I followed Anna around, Mike was sitting in his highchair eating cereal and watching a children's program on TV. Anna was drinking coffee and reading the paper in the dining alcove nearby. Michael showed me his room, which is gaily decorated with pictures made with cloth material (done by Anna, I believe). The shelves and toy chest are overflowing with toys. Before Robert left, a little before 8:00 A.M., he came to say goodbye to Michael, spending a few minutes talking with him.

In the evening, when Anna and I return from her office, the first thing Michael asks when we come in the door is: "What did you bring me today?" His parents often bring something when they come home, Anna explains. Robert has brought him a book that day. Anna likes to be with Michael when she comes home from work. She encourages him to help her make dinner while I am watching. He washes the lettuce for the salad and sets the table, with some supervision from his mother. The house is "childproofed"; no breakable objects are within his reach. The edges of the glass table have protectors on them so he can't hurt himself if he falls against them.

Anna's face always lights up when she talks about Mike. At the office she has some of his artwork on the wall next to her desk. The pictures are placed so low that one cannot easily see them when entering her office, but she has a picture of Michael prominently displayed. Her secretary tells me that when Mary had an emergency, Anna brought Michael to the office. Everybody looked after him. They were not used to having a child around and enjoyed him. He was also content playing by himself part of the time. His father came around 1:00 P.M. to pick him up. Her boss is very understanding, Anna relates, since he has a young child of his own whom he stayed at home to care for between jobs. Anna certainly has no reluctance to talk about Michael with her colleagues when introducing me, telling them about the topic of my research, always mentioning the ages of their children and encouraging them to tell me about their situations. Her freedom in talking about her child is in contrast to the silence of some of the others who hesitate to advertise their motherhood.

Another day, when I stop by Anna's office to talk, she has just returned from a few days' trip. She tells me with obvious pleasure how happy Michael had been when she came home. She does not feel guilty about working, she says. "Michael is coming along very well." She truly has difficulty understanding how women can stay home all the time. Many of her old friends did so for a few years after their children were born. She notes that a psychologist friend of theirs gave up work entirely when she had a child. "I wonder what she does with herself all day long."

Catherine returned to work ten weeks after Steve was born. "It's a real change in your life, and I wanted to find out what it was like to have a baby before I turned him over to someone else's care." She would have liked some more time, she notes, but was comfortable with the time she had. She hired through an agency a live-out housekeeper who turned out to be excellent. Before her comprehensive exam, Catherine was studying two evenings a week and on weekends. In the country she had a baby sitter to whom she took Steve. "It was a nice situation," she says, because the woman had a child one year older than Steve. She still studies in the evening twice weekly at the office. She finds the atmosphere more conducive to study there. Because George didn't feel comfortable taking care of Steve when he was a baby, Catherine hired a baby nurse for the evenings she studied. Now George takes care of Steve on those evenings and when she travels every other month. "George's job is nine to five and he never travels."

Steve is a healthy child and Catherine hasn't taken any time off from work. She thinks that if he had been sickly, George would have shared staying home with Steve to some extent, but she would have done most of it. She wouldn't have lost her job, but her career would have suffered. That's her "judgment of what reality is." Secretaries in her firm do it with no negative consequences, but at her level of responsibility it is different, she thinks. She trusts her housekeeper and will take time off only if Steve has a high fever.

When Catherine became pregnant, she told herself she had better go to the mother's group that she had read about in the organization newsletter and find out what she could from them. "It's been helpful. The women at work have children the same age as Steve, so they can't tell much of what to anticipate, but we get together for lunch and talk on the phone about problems." She does research on baby care as methodically as she does her work. She reads, investigates, purposefully talks with other mothers about what to expect, and compares the various opinions.

At the time of this interview, Catherine tells me her current project is to find a play group for Steve. She wants him to get out at least twice a week in the fall to be with other children, especially during the winter because Lillian, the housekeeper, is not keen on going out when it is cold.

Catherine's usual day with Steve starts around 7:00 A.M. She gives him a bottle while she has coffee and reads the *New York Times*. She interacts with him "more or less" as he is playing and she is reading. She leaves for work when Lillian arrives at 8:30 A.M. "Lillian is excellent at housekeeping. The house is always neat. She feeds Steve dinner before I come home." His bedtime is 8–8:30 P.M. (Steve is fourteen months old at the time of this interview.)

When Catherine comes home in the evening, the time is pretty much Steve's. "When he was little, there wasn't much he could do." Now that he can walk, the two of them go for a walk with a nearby park as their destination. "That's concentrated time and that's all his."

Catherine describes Steve's day with Lillian. They go to the park in the summer and to the store. He loves that. He has an engaging smile, and people like to interact with him. She is very pleased with the way Lillian helps him advance. She encourages him to feed himself, for example. Catherine has observed how patiently she does this. She and Lillian don't spend a good deal of time discussing what should be done next. "He likes Lillian a lot. . . . He has become more attached to me now. When he was six months, he didn't notice my comings and goings." Catherine comments that she hasn't had any major problems with extended crying when she leaves in the morning.

George told Catherine that his sons, although their mother stayed home, always had lots of nurses and maids.

He said it will be all right; they always distinguish mother from maid. I was never worried about that. [She obviously has discussed it.] That's one thing [worrying] that didn't happen. That happens to a lot of women, but not to me. My psychological makeup is such that I don't spend an excessive amount of time worrying about the ability to be a mother. I look around. About 90 percent of women are mothers. They are of all levels of intelligence, all levels of ability, all levels of energy. Sometimes their children turn out, sometimes they don't. It's not necessarily related to how much time and effort they put in. So I don't spend a lot of time analyzing whether I am a good mother or a bad mother. I feel I will be an adequate mother. I am certainly going to try very hard.

Catherine says that even though she has rearranged many things, there still is a lot more work to do with a child around. She is much more efficient now, she thinks. There is a limit to the amount of time available to make up for any procrastination by working late, she comments.

Catherine was an avid tennis player and backpacker before Steve was born. She has given that up completely but is looking forward to the time Steve can do sports with them. She and George are very sports oriented. That will be what she views as quality time. "You can spend time with him and see his abilities increase, and we will have the opportunity to interact as a family. It will be fun and we can do it together."

Catherine goes on to discuss Steve's schooling:

What is preying on my mind now is the whole school thing. I consider private schools too snooty an environment. I don't think public schooling quality is good enough. Hunter is fine, but that depends entirely on him, his intelligence, etc. Something I can't count on. I have to find people who live in Manhattan who can tell me of the characteristics of private schools here so I can minimize things that I consider negative, to select which one to send him to, but I think that's going to be a very time-consuming proposition.

Steve is an adorable looking boy. Eighteen months old when I visited, he is active and friendly. Catherine kept an eye on him while talking. Both parents admonished him at times and prevented him from doing damage to things around him. The house was not completely "childproofed" for him. George talked to him like a friend. He assembles all Steve's toys, his tricycles, for example. Steve has two of them, one for the country and one for the city. George commented that he is surprised how well things are working out with Steve:

One is fine. I wouldn't recommend it on an income of $30,000. There is a critical mass of money that is an essential ingredient in getting through this comfortably. It's a lot of fun when you are 22 years old, when you have energy coming out of your ears. Then you can bear with it.

When Sandy returned to work, the severity of Elizabeth's condition was as yet not apparent, although it had been noted in the hospital and was followed closely by the doctor afterward. Sandy's housekeeper would take Elizabeth to the doctor's office and Sandy would join them there. After Elizabeth was hospitalized when she was two or three months' old, the housekeeper would arrive at the hospital when Sandy left for work after visiting her daughter in the morning. Sandy would go over at lunch time and then after work, when her housekeeper left for home. She herself left in the evening. She felt that for her own sanity's sake it was better to go home for the night. This was a rough period, which Sandy doesn't like to talk about; when she does, it is with a shudder. Only in bits and pieces does one find out about her infant daughter first being in traction, then in a body cast that had to be changed as she grew.

Sandy was also reluctant to discuss her daughter's situation at work, not wanting anyone to downgrade her abilities or to let her concern interfere with her work. She admits that this was the only time in her professional life when she didn't do as good a job in her work as she knew she could, although she obviously did well enough to earn her vice presidency. When she returned to work, she had been given a job once removed from a line position, but with good exposure and located near the area's executive vice president, for whom she had great respect. She met Richard in this office when Elizabeth was nine months old. She liked the project she was on, but it wouldn't take her anywhere as fast as she wanted to go. She resented the protection her female boss was extending to her both before and after Elizabeth's birth, talking rather disdainfully of her boss's views that she should not be under stress because of her "delicate condition" and, later, motherhood. Richard told her that her boss was trying to be nice. By now he had become her mentor, and was at the same level as her boss. Sandy felt she learned a lot about office politics from Richard and in a sense had access to the "old boys' network" through him. No one at work knew they were going out together. Sandy was ready to move on. After a year when her project was finished, she went back to a line position, in charge of a regional area with 13 offices. Richard moved on elsewhere.

By this time Sandy had changed housekeepers because she thought the first one too young. She did not have complete trust in her. When Elizabeth was seven months old, she found Charlene, who is still with them. She lived in at first, as did the first one. After her two teenagers were brought to the United States a year ago, Charlene got an apartment and now sleeps over only when needed in the evening.

When Sandy and Richard started living together after about two years, his children visited every other weekend and once during the week, frequently more often. Sandy had to adjust to becoming a stepmother as well. She read every book she could find on the subject. "Some were very helpful," she says; "it could be rough." Actually this situation brought her to the organization's Mothers' Group. Sandy and Richard married a little over a year ago. He is now legally adopting Elizabeth. Soon there will be two children around regularly, and four a good deal of the time.

Charlene tells of how easy Elizabeth was to take care of. She never cried or complained about the "harness" she had to be in at all times except when taking a bath. Her dress covered it up. She could move but was restricted. Charlene doesn't remember when the harness came off, but believes Elizabeth wore it for about a year. Charlene extols Sandy in many ways, especially as a mother.

She would be with Elizabeth every chance she had. She would go to school at night too and yet she would get up at night for Elizabeth. She told me she would attend to her. She made it her duty to get up every morning and make breakfast for Elizabeth. When she didn't go to class, she would meet me at the park and tell me to go home. She really was with the child a lot, considering all the work she had to do. Sandy is hardly ever sick.

Charlene describes her fondly as a "tough little lady." She describes Elizabeth similarly.

She never had any trouble after her harness was removed. She acts as if it never happened. She's very tough. She would go to the big slides [in the park], she wasn't afraid. She has a lot of her mother in her. . . . She has lots of friends. They often come over to play for a few hours. She visits them too. Elizabeth loved nursery school.

Charlene would take her there. Charlene goes on to talk about what Sandy does now. For example, she often takes Elizabeth to school, and visits the school when Elizabeth is performing. She takes time off from work and makes it up in the evening. She makes time if she wants to talk to the teacher about something. Sandy always takes over when she comes home from work. She and Elizabeth tell each other about their day. They may go out for an ice cream. When Richard comes home, they will all chat. If Sandy feels like it, she cooks dinner. "She loves cooking. Richard is a good cook too, he helps." Sometimes they order food in. If Richard comes home before Sandy and Charlene wants to leave, he takes charge. He has taken over making breakfast for Elizabeth. "It's a habit. Sandy expects him to and he does." During the work week, Charlene gives Elizabeth a bath after dinner, which the two of them eat together. She puts Elizabeth in her pajamas. Sandy and Richard eat too late for Elizabeth.

There is evidence of Sandy and Elizabeth's projects in the apartment. Easter eggs are on the dining room table. Charlene tells me that they were done in the country. Other creations of theirs hang in the living room.

There are rules for the children in the house. When I have dinner with them, Elizabeth proudly brings in the hors d'oeuvres. Richard explains to me that she has been given the privilege of participating in our talk until her bedtime, between 8:00–9:00 P.M. He also tells her that she mustn't interrupt conversations. Yet she is responded to and very much a part of the discussion. She is also told that she can't sit in Richard's chair, and she removes herself immediately when he wants to sit down. She laughs and says, "I forgot." This appears to be a family-focused house, where everybody's rights are respected. The child's wishes do not necessarily come first. She somewhat reluctantly goes off to bed; both parents are firm about this. Sandy promises to read her a story when she has finished the main course. The dinner was made by Sandy. She takes pains to explain that she has not done it all herself. Charlene has bought the chicken and prepared it. All she had to do was to put it in the oven.

Elizabeth has many activities. Charlene says, "She seems to thrive on them." She goes to "movement" class at the "Y" and is included in a group of about five children who go once a week to the home of a kindergarten classmate whose mother is French. They play and talk in French. Elizabeth recites numbers in French for us. Elizabeth also visits her grandparents in the suburbs. When I talked with Charlene on a Monday, she was expecting them to bring her home after a long weekend visit.

Elizabeth is a charming, bright little girl, now 5 years old. Sandy told me some time ago that the one thing in the world she would not know how to cope with would be anything happening to Elizabeth. She gave as an example of her feeling overcautious in fastening Elizabeth into her car seat; she will check and recheck and still be worried. Her family teases her about her behavior.

I first met Karin and her children at a brunch. Lise was happily sitting at the table with the grown-ups, getting a lot of attention. She is a friendly, beautiful little girl, 2 years old, with big blue eyes and a frequent smile. Marcel, now four months old, was asleep for a good part of the time.

Karin has very definite ideas as to what kind of mother she wants to be to her children. She follows her own ideas with great determination, no matter how tired she is. She probably would brush aside this description somewhat impatiently with a "no big deal" statement. What has to be done, has to be done. She wants to spend time with both her children and makes certain Lise has special time with her. She gets up to nurse Marcel twice during the night. This will soon be eased when he will need only one feeding. She is beginning to wean him. She changes both children in the morning, getting up at 7:00 A.M., and has breakfast with Lise and one of her grandparents, while Marcel sits in a highchair by the table or she holds him in one arm. Lise will want to sit on her lap. Somewhere here she tries to read the paper and discuss dinner plans with her parent. Barbara, the housekeeper, arrives at 8:30 and Karin leaves for work. Somehow she manages to get dressed, because she leaves when Barbara arrives. Lise will often walk with her to the elevator. Barbara or her grandparent takes her back and distracts her should she cry.

Karin used to work until 9:00 or 10:00 P.M. three times weekly. She does not do this now, while the children are young. She evidently does not have to work abroad for the time being. Neither does she travel now. It isn't clear to me whether this will hamper her career. She frequently takes reading material for work home with her. She doesn't view this as work, unless she has to write a report. Actually, the way I calculate it, she could at the utmost squeeze in only one hour's work in the evening. That is between the time she puts Lise to bed and says goodbye to guests and the time she feeds Marcel, changes diapers, and falls into bed herself. It certainly would make a big difference if her husband were here on a daily basis. The other alternative would be to have a sleep-in housekeeper, but she doesn't have the room.

Karin also makes it clear that she would not want to spend all her time with the children. She loves her career. She says, "I have no guilt feelings about going to work. I probably spend as much time with the children as a mother who stays home."

Karin hasn't taken sick leave since she went back to work after Marcel was born. She tells me she was sick one weekend with a high temperature. Her mother wasn't feeling well either. How did she manage? "You just function. You can't just lie down and let everybody die around you," she laughs.

The day I followed Karin around, Lise had had diarrhea during the night. By morning it had subsided. Karin's mother had taken care of Lise so that Karin didn't know anything about it until morning. She is concerned and gives thorough, detailed instructions to Barbara. When we get to the subway station, Karin is almost visibly shifting gears, beginning to think about work. She takes out her calendar, saying she would normally do this at home to make certain that she brought all her papers with her. This morning she was too preoccupied with Lise. When Karin returns home about 6:00

P.M., the children have her complete attention. She first nurses Marcel, then sits down to a dinner prepared by her parent. She then goes for a walk with Lise. If the weather is bad, they run up and down corridors and staircases playing. Then she plays with both children, preferably on the terrace. Their sublet apartment has a huge terrace with a children's play swing, a wading pool, etc. They sing and dance. Karin has taught Lise some nursery songs in her native language. Three languages are spoken in the house.

Karin says, "If they are happy, everything is so much easier." This is in answer to my comment about the amount of energy involved in all this activity. Karin gives Lise a bath, teaching her in the process how to undress. They get done in time for all of them to sit down and look at the "Muppet" show on TV. Marcel is put to bed when he is sleepy and Lise at 8:30–9:00 P.M. Karin reads her a story before she goes to sleep. Her mother tells me that Andre takes over many of these tasks when he is there, such as diapering, putting one of them to bed, etc.

During the day Barbara takes Lise to the park or to visit with friends. Lise will be starting in a private nursery program in the fall, two half-days a week. When Karin is late, as she was, for example, when she went looking for apartments, Barbara will stay until she returns. She is paid extra for this.

Karin takes the children with her everywhere she goes. When Andre is not there, she often has friends over, not more than one or two people at a time. When Andre comes home, they always go out alone to catch up with each other. Their long-distance telephone bill is quite heavy. They also socialize a good deal when he is there.

As can be seen, my informants have very different mothering styles. The children are obviously an immensely important part of their lives. It seems equally clear that in the way they manage their pregnancies and their children, their careers are paramount. They attempt to balance their prior-

ities between their careers and their children. As reality will
have it, the job demands their presence; their children are
in the hands of good caretakers of their choice. Some spend
more time with their children and others more with their
work, depending on the demands of the job and their own
needs. If they want to move up the ladder, the demands
are great, just as they are for men. Society has not made
any convenient arrangements for the women. They are finding their own solution. The children manage.

The preliminary research finding that children are not
adversely affected by their mothers' working—as Zimmerman and Bernstein (1983), for example, suggest—is what
my informants tend to believe. It is notable, therefore, that
the report of the above study was received with some skep-
ticism by several women at a meeting, in contrast to their
usual optimism. Remarks such as "Let's wait and see until
they reach adolescence" were heard mixed with the more
positive ones. These doubts most likely stem from their own
concern about the effect their careers and their child rearing
have on their children.

Basically, however, as with everything else, they follow the
credo of the success subculture: if something is important,
they can do something about it. The children are important,
so they set about learning as much as possible about child
rearing and child development to enable them to do the best
they can with their children—hence the many speakers on
these topics at the Working Mothers' luncheons. As mentioned, they also get affirmation that they are doing the right
thing. Beyond that, they feel, there is nothing more they can
do. As Catherine put it, "I feel I will be an adequate mother.
I am certainly going to try very hard." Her psychological makeup
is such, she says, that she doesn't spend time analyzing whether
she is a good mother. This is the key to how she and the
other women handle most situations in life.

They will do any number of things, mainly at their own
expense, not to jeopardize their careers or their children. If

something were desperately wrong with a child, requiring their leaving their careers temporarily, I think they would do so. On a day-to-day basis the job must of necessity come first for them, and here is where their many support systems come in.

They believe they are better mothers for going to work. They are stimulated by their work and think they can give more to their children. They do not advocate this path for everyone, only for those who want to be allowed to compete in the labor market along with men without stereotyping. Societal pressure to stay home with the child in the early years is still evident, but staying at home does not necessarily make women better mothers with happier children. There is plenty of evidence to the contrary. Betty Friedan elaborated on this at length in *The Feminine Mystique*. "Good" or "bad" mothers can be found in any segment of society, working or "nonworking." It is for the mothers who want to stay home but cannot for economic reasons that we should be concerned. Yet, Baruch, Barnett, and Rivers (1983:155) found that this concern may not be warranted. They write:

One intriguing finding from our study was that even if an employed woman preferred to be home, that conflict didn't have a significant impact on her well-being. But a homemaker who was at home when she wanted to be at work suffered serious consequences to well-being. The woman who is at home out of feminine "duty" is in trouble. The woman who is there because she wants to be is apt to be pleased with her life.

The career women's main strategy around child care is delegation of responsibilities and tasks. Society has demanded for a long time that everything should be done by the all-nurturing mother. My informants use support systems instead in many areas that are deemed by many to be only the mother's territory. The housekeeper emerges as the women's number one practical and concrete support in regard to the children. The husbands come next; they support both practically and emotionally. They complete the circle, making everything right in their world if they are supportive, as the husbands in my study are. I consider their support a vital ingredient in these social systems. But the housekeeper is the main factor in making possible the career women's success. There are, of course, other kinds of caretakers, such as extended family. These are not available to most of the women, nor would day-care centers be very practical for some of them because of the women's irregular hours, even if they were available.

The problems of parents in arranging child care when a full-time housekeeper is not used are vividly described in Kamerman's (1980) *Parenting in an Unresponsive Society: Managing Work and Family Life*. She writes:

Just the logistics of the child care for one child, let alone two or more children, often seemed overwhelming as we heard mother after mother describe multiple and complicated arrangements requiring planning, organization, and reliability. Indeed, one of the most difficult aspects of this approach to child care, as one mother told us, is the "linkage" problem—in other words, getting a child from home to a preschool program, when the program begins after the mother has to leave for her job, or arranging for a child to go from kindergarten to a family day care mother or a relative's home for afternoon care. (1980:36)

Kamerman notes that "parental ingenuity and creativeness are extraordinary, with parents sometimes selecting complicated work schedules in order to provide a significant portion of child care themselves" (1980:36). She found that "among two-parent professional families [in the study population], the use of paid domestic help is the dominant child care mode in one-third of the families and is used as part of a child care package by about one-half" (Kamerman 1980:45).

For many people, then, household help is the most convenient and favored form of child care when both parents work and they can afford it. My informants certainly have found it so.

The theme that emerges quite clearly is that my informants cannot conceive of themselves staying home with the children all the time. They need to be involved in work outside the home. Sandy again, with her inimitable frankness, relates at a meeting: "My husband says I have a ten-day limit. After that I am a danger to my child." Many quotations in the preceding pages indicate that she is not alone. On the other side of the coin, the enormous gratification they get from their children is equally clear. One characteristic remark that I heard from one woman after another, both informants and others, went something like this: "You know, when I leave my office, I begin to anticipate seeing my child. The closer I get to my house, the faster I walk. I usually end up running the last half of the block."

If one views the successful career women who are also mothers as general managers, the theme running through their stories back up the contention that the core department in their "companies" is the career, around which the family has to adjust itself. They also confirm my major point that success cannot be attained and maintained by one person alone. Career women require a sustaining crowd. There is ample evidence of this in the story of each of my informants. Numerous other support systems, apart from the housekeepers and husbands, have been mentioned, such as neighbors, friends, and even a chairman of the board. All play a role in making the systems viable. The women use their managerial skills in organizing the care of their children, intertwining these skills with reward systems which ensure that the best possible care is given.

6

The "Green Card Ladies" and the Nursemaid

SUSIE, RON, MAGGIE SMITH

130 Central Park West
New York City
Phone #

2 Ocean Drive
West Hampton, L.I.
Phone #

WE WISH TO FIND:

A self sufficient person to care for our independent 3 year old.

COMPENSATION:

• Earn $175 a week with no room and board expenses

• Live at 81st Street next to Central Park, the Museum of Natural History, across the park from Metropolitan Museum of Art (we have membership in both), churches, shops . . . everything within walking distance. Live in large bedroom with TV and private bath.

• Weekends free or come to the country (West Hampton, L.I.) with us and have your own duplex apartment and use of a car.

• Most evenings free—take a class at the museums, go to one of dozens of movies, join church group.

• Two weeks vacation.

RESPONSIBILITIES—In general, care for Maggie

- Take Maggie to school in morning and pick her up at noon.

- Arrange and supervise play with other children in afternoon.

- Prepare meals for Maggie and light dinner for all of us in evenings.

- Miscellaneous household tasks, e.g., grocery shopping, wash, etc.

SITUATION:

Mother and father both work in Manhattan and travel occasionally. We wish to find a mature person with whom we can confidently leave Maggie and who will enjoy her company.

One person (Rosie) and her husband have lived with us since Maggie was born. She will move to Texas at the end of June to join the rest of her family.

We wish to develop a similar long term and caring relationship with a person as responsible as Rosie has been.

This memorandum was deposited with the Working Mothers' group to enlist their help in finding a housekeeper. It is not atypical, and many housekeepers have been found through this kind of networking. Those who do not live in earn around $250 to $275 a week with social security paid. The housekeeper is the precious person to whom the career women entrust their children and without whom they cannot function in the long run. As we have just seen, the housekeeper is literally the main component in their social system, their main support. The women are aware of this and will go to quite some length to compensate and reward her. If the housekeeper is a "green card lady" (an alien legitimately here with a working permit), the career women may sponsor her children or other family members to come to the United States, as Sandy did. Kitty lent her housekeeper money for furniture. "We don't even have all our own furniture yet," she comments.

Many do not want a live-in housekeeper because of the personal closeness and involvement this entails. Nevertheless, they obviously do get quite involved. Those who travel and have extensive business activities in the evening forgo their privacy in order to have a sleep-in housekeeper available at all times. Most of the women spend time with their housekeepers, ascertaining that they are all right, discussing their problems with them.

Charlene is a pleasant, somewhat reticent and shy woman in her late thirties. Sandy has learned the signs that tell when Charlene wants to talk, and Sandy discusses Charlene's children with her.

Sandy's approach to those who work for her is to tell them, "Take charge. If you don't want to do that, don't take this job. If you want me to tell you what to do every day, you don't belong here." That goes for business as well as home.

When Charlene started to work for Sandy, she was taken to the kitchen and told to take over and buy and/or eat anything she wanted. Sandy keeps the "cookie jar" full of money. Charlene could never run out. Sandy doesn't want to see any bills and tells Charlene that she has confidence in her and also that she is too frugal. Charlene says, "My job is to look after Elizabeth. I do the laundry, some light cleaning. I run the house, do some shopping, but make dinner only for Elizabeth and myself."

Sandy believes that she is extremely supportive of people working for her who have personal problems at home. She tells them to go home and take care of themselves. If things aren't taken care of and their support is breaking down, she becomes less tolerant. Then she steps in and coaches her workers.

If Charlene's kids are sick for five days and haven't seen a doctor, I want to know why. I am a terrible taskmaster. I am very critical of something that isn't done right. In the long run that also gains them prestige, working with someone like me. I remember Charlene when she started working for me. She would immediately start talking to the man delivering the groceries about the man in the house, despite the fact we didn't have one, so as not to give the feeling that there are delicate little ladies around here. I don't think she has that kind of insecurity anymore. We are taken care of whether there is a man or not.

This is the "I" talking. Sandy wants her sustaining crowd to know they are secure when she is around, and she also wants them to function at their optimum when she is away. The strategies she employs are what a "good manager" would use to have his/her organization function smoothly to get the desired output.

Charlene tells me, for example, that if Sandy has a day off, she gives Charlene the day off. "I don't work when she doesn't work." Charlene often thinks of how she got her job. It was not advertised in the paper. It was fate, according to Charlene. A friend of Sandy's had interviewed Charlene and passed the news on to Sandy.

Charlene speaks of herself with some pride. Sandy tells her she is the most important person in the house, which both pleases and embarrasses Charlene. Charlene feels that she must have some of Sandy's personality characteristics because they get along so well. She notes that "Elizabeth considers me part of the family. Whenever she draws a picture of the family, I am always part of it."

Charlene now wants to move on and get a job with a future. She would like health and dental insurance for herself and the children. Sandy and Richard are trying very hard to help her with this. She has been with Sandy over five years now, and they are in complete accord with her wish to move on. Interestingly, Sandy cannot comprehend how Charlene could leave her children in the West Indies when she came here. One might wonder what she would have done with her own drive and ambition if she had been in the same position. Sandy doesn't really see the privileged position she was in when she started. She thinks that she herself is the one who will feel the loss the most when Charlene leaves. Elizabeth will be able to see her often, since Charlene will continue to live nearby.

Karin tells me she always asks a question when interviewing for a housekeeper: "What is the difference in the way you bring up children in your country and the way they do it in the United States?" She finds it the most helpful and informative one in terms of getting the applicants to expand on how they handle children in general. She liked the way Barbara answered this question, and that she was not too young. Indeed, all my informants prefer their housekeepers not to be too young. Barbara has turned out to be just what Karin wanted. She handles the children with "little discipline, but a lot of talk and play." Karin describes Barbara as smart, energetic, reliable, and caring. She reflects on Barbara's job:

I have thought about that. Funny job, she loves Lise and I think she is jealous of me. If Lise should cry when I leave, she has told me, "Lise must love you very much because she cries when you leave." She doesn't cry when Barbara leaves because I am there. Actually, I felt I had to pull back in my mothering when I was at home. Her entire job satisfaction is love.

There is a certain incredulity in Karin's voice as she talks. She adds, "She really needs empathy. It's like she's the wife staying home to look after the children and I'm the breadwinner who goes to work and has an interesting time."

Karin says she got to know Barbara very well when she stayed at home on her materntiy leave. Barbara is divorced and has two teenage daughters, living with her here in New York. Barbara too is from the West Indies. Because Karin liked Barbara's wanting to improve her situation, she took the time to tutor her so that she could obtain her high school diploma. Karin comments somewhat resignedly,

She is pregnant now, and I guess that's the way she wants to handle her life. She was finally in a position where she could have been free to go on with her career and life. I guess she wants to be dependent. She is 38 years old, and having a baby now with a married man is not going to make things work out any other way. He apparently wants to take care of her. He doesn't have any children.

That situation, according to Karin's understanding, is not unusual in the culture Barbara comes from. The man will openly have a relationship with a woman who will bear him a child. This means that Karin has to find another house-keeper in 3 to 4 months. Even so, Karin plans to pay Barbara in full when Karin and her family are away on vacation for a month.

Kitty's new housekeeper, the sister of another organiza-tion member's housekeeper, is also from the Caribbean. It was rather a shock to Kitty when her last housekeeper didn't show up one day and had contradictory stories about the reasons for it. Kitty had had great confidence in her.

Kitty relates that Bridgit is taking well to the new house-keeper, Helene, who is warm and caring. Her previous housekeeper was firmer with Bridgit, and Kitty feels that Helene is letting her get away with more than she should. Kitty is talking to her about this. The fact that Helene does light cooking for them before she leaves in the evening is a real break for Kitty. Helene refuses to prepare the menus, however; so Kitty still does that herself. Helene has a 5-year-old child who is cared for after school by Helene's sister.

I had noted at meetings that the majority of the women have "green card ladies." Catherine and Anna are excep-tions. Catherine's housekeeper comes from the South, and Anna's nursemaid from Ireland; and their two relationships do not seem to be as close as the others'. Catherine actually sees Lillian very little. She talks with Lillian briefly in the morning, and Lillian leaves shortly after Catherine returns in the evening. As a matter of fact, George believes that the less involvement with the help, the better. He says he learned this from past experience. There always seemed to be some difficult entanglement between his ex-wife and the help. When he wants something done, he always routes the request through Catherine. This is in contrast with Sandy and Richard. If Richard tells Sandy, for example, that he doesn't have any clean socks, her response is, "Don't tell me, tell Charlene." The two different styles of interacting with the housekeeper are obviously idiosyncratic and geared to individual needs. One could speculate that Lillian, born in this country, has more friends and family here than Charlene, for instance. In short, she has her own support systems and doesn't need the personal involvement many of the "green card ladies" seem to invite.

Anna and Mary may talk more than I am aware of, but, as noted earlier, there is more of an established code of behavior for nursemaids than for housekeepers. Anna had to persuade her to make a simple dinner on the days Michael goes to school. Mary has many friends who are nursemaids, and I believe that preparing dinner is not a task within their code.

Mary, who appears to be about 40 years old, has been in the United States for seventeen years but speaks with a distinct Irish brogue. She is a pleasant woman, immaculately dressed in blouse and skirt. The word that comes to mind when one talks of Mary is "proper." She started as a babynurse. This generally means very short jobs and sleeping in. It also means getting up frequently during the night. Mary therefore prefers being a nursemaid. She has held two jobs at the same time, but found this nerve-wracking.

Mary sees her role, aside from looking after Michael, as one of teaching him manners, getting him to dress himself and to put his things away, and teaching him how to occupy himself. She talks about the English nannies who are very "tough" on manners and discipline. Apparently she is not so strict.

Mary and her Irish cronies congregate around the Hans Christian Andersen statue in the wintertime, as do the Scottish and English nursemaids, but they generally sit in groups by nationality. Mary laughingly says, "We do mingle sometimes, but the English nannies are very cliquish." At a certain time all the groups go up to the playground for 20 to 30 minutes. This is where the West Indians sit all the time.

Mary has some family here, mostly upstate, and doesn't see them very often. The nursemaids frequently share apartments. Mary says she has lots of friends. She prefers to sit with those in the park who don't always talk about children. That gets tiresome.

Most nursemaids expect to leave a job when the children reach kindergarten or school age. "You can always find another job. Besides it gets boring, so you like to move on." Clearly, being a nursemaid is Mary's profession. She has no desire to do anything else for the rest of her life, nor any intention of changing. It would seem that Mary and her cronies are more professional in their attitude and in their thinking about themselves than the housekeepers. They view themselves as higher in the pecking order than the West Indians. Racial prejudice, I am certain, plays a part in this. Realistically, however, they are not so dependent on their employers as the "green card ladies," who have more problems with their families still at home in the West Indies and the need to establish themselves here. The nursemaids have more options, more opportunities for work, and do not get so emotionally involved. These factors have implications for the career women in terms of their own needs. It seems highly unlikely that the nursemaids would accept the kind of irregular and demanding schedule required by the very busy career women. They would have to hire several nursemaids at the same time. (I understand that some women do.) This would, of course, cause further management problems.

A caretaker of a child can be in a powerful position. If she and the child get along well, one may be willing to overlook many things. Sometimes this situation can get out of hand. One woman stated flatly at one of the Mothers' Group meetings that her housekeeper controlled the household. They had let her get away with it because their "child simply adored her." She was told in no uncertain terms what to do about the situation and left this particular luncheon determined to straighten things out.

Jean illustrates the case of the inflexible baby nurse. Hers was an English one,

who was terrific with my child. She knew lots of things about babies that I didn't know. She was inflexible. She wanted to leave the house at six. I didn't have that kind of job. Months went by and I had a boss at the time who was in the habit of calling me in at the end of the day, reviewing it. My stomach would be in my throat, knowing [that] she wanted to leave. Finally my mother-in-law, who is a wonderful woman, took me aside one Sunday, [and said] "This woman is great for the baby, but not for you. You've got to get rid of her." But she is honest, reliable, etc. [Mother-in-law]: "So are a million others. Get someone else." So I did. Hired a woman who is with us now. She sleeps in. . . . [In the] last couple of years she has averaged three nights in. She is full time now with the new baby.

The conclusion to be drawn from this discussion is that a baby nurse or a housekeeper who has her own life to lead does not do very well in the household of the successful career woman who travels and does business in the evening. In order to manage, she herself would have to establish the same kind of adaptable support systems that the career women have.

Because the housekeeper is in charge of the child's well being and has power and leverage, there is a greater interdependence in the relationship between the career women and the housekeeper than in the usual employer-employee relationship. The career women will go to great lengths to ensure that the housekeeper is content and will therefore in turn function well in her job as her major support system. If personal problems interfere, she will try to counsel. The two women do establish relationships that can be both close and caring, but ultimately their own and the child's well-being rests on the housekeeper's sense of well-being. As Gilligan (1982:63) writes about human experience, "We know ourselves as separate only insofar as we live in connection with others, and . . . we experience relationship only insofar as we differentiate other from self." Each woman seems to learn through experience and advice where to draw the line when her own input into making the housekeeper happy is not cost-effective anymore. The basic requirement for the career woman's housekeeper is that she take care of the child and be available whenever needed. The standards set for the rest, such as housekeeping, meal-cooking, laundry, etc., are much less vital. Most career women have additional cleaning help anyway.

Those women who employ the more professional nurse-maids, who aren't available at all times, need additional help if they do not keep regular working hours. The "green card lady" is, figuratively speaking, as much of a slave to the career woman with irregular hours as the career woman is to her work.

Other researchers have pointed out that the career women reach and maintain their success on the backs of these women who are the caretakers of their children. "One class of women escaped some of the constraints of sex stratification through utilization of the labor of the class of women most severely limited by it" (Hunt and Hunt 1982:44). In reality, therefore, the Hunts point out, there is little deviation from the conventional domestic division of labor in using a housekeeper.

There seems little sense in arguing this ironic fact. I see no solutions except changing the economic system in which we live or enabling people through a combination of political and other societal forces to have more opportunities. The career women themselves are the recipients of new opportunities obtained through such a process. There is evidence, at least among my informants, that the career women make an effort to help their housekeepers progress socioeconomically if those housekeepers are interested in doing so.

An interesting aspect of the women's use of housekeepers is their apparent ability to have their children cared for by caretakers without feeling the heavy burden of guilt that so many other women appear to carry around. Except for Karin and Anna, none of my informants had a socialization process in which household help figured. The reasons for this apparent lack of guilt are manifold and have been outlined in various ways throughout these pages. Briefly, as I see it, the women are convinced of their right to realize themselves, and that they are happier women because of it. Furthermore, they believe that balancing their energies and time between their careers and their children makes them "better" mothers. Their strong self-confidence underpins these beliefs. The only way these objectives can be accomplished is through delegating part of their mothering role. The role models of their socialization process, even though different, nevertheless encouraged most of my informants to achieve and to forge new roles for themselves as career women and mothers in our changing times. The women are pragmatic, down-to-earth people who see the housekeeper as a good solution to the problem of caring for their children when they or the fathers are not around. It is therefore with relatively little guilt that they use a housekeeper.

The reality is that my informants have all chosen full-time housekeepers as their preference in the care of their children. They can afford it. The women also have more choice and control in regard to a housekeeper who performs a great many functions apart from taking care of their children in a way they approve. The housekeeper affords them peace of mind and makes things more comfortable for them and their families. Her presence eliminates many of the complications Kamerman (1980) describes. In that way the housekeeper is an indispensable tool in the women's lives and social systems, and they know it. The housekeeper is replaceable, of course, but only with someone of the women's choice. I am reminded of Sandy's comment at a meeting: "When Richard asked me to marry him, I told him I had to check with Charlene first, if she approved." Richard is reported to have told Charlene what Sandy had said, adding, "She meant it."

7

Social Activity and The Country House

My informants differ greatly from one another in the ways they deal with the many aspects of life and career. So do they differ when it comes to their social activities, whether business entertaining or socializing with family and friends. They all have to fit their activities, work and nonwork, into the twenty-four hours of the day. To maintain their success, they have to do a certain number of things under their own steam; others are done with the help of others. Priorities are idiosyncratic. Many women say that socializing is one of the first things to be cut drastically when the children are born, a statement I accept with reservations. What seems like a large amount of activity to one career woman may seem like nothing to another. It is with this in mind that I will look at my informants' social activity.

The more work-focused person will, of course, do more business entertaining than others. Some do both business and personal entertaining at home. Others concentrate on family and friends in their off-work activities and do their business entertaining at breakfast and lunch.

It may be instructive to look first at a woman who seems to be at the far end of the spectrum in terms of activities and energy. Jean (pilot study) is such a person. She is perhaps the most overtly ambitious, and she is very proud of her accomplishments. Even though she is not one of my informants, I have talked with her extensively and heard her in meetings. She is viewed by her professional women friends as the "superwoman." She does more than most, works longer hours and travels more, they think. Some marvel and some snipe at her drive. "She can manage on 4–5 hours sleep," they remark. "I couldn't do that." Actually Jean says, she gets about six hours sleep. "I have a friend," she laughs, "who strongly believes that 'Anyone who sleeps more than four hours is in dress rehearsal for the final sleep.'" Jean believes emphatically that energy is a learned skill. She also believes in getting mileage out of each day. She proclaims that she enjoys everything she does. She starts her day at 5:00 A.M. and winds down like a clock at the end of the day. She says she is "as healthy as a horse." She may be out as often as four or five weekday evenings, with her husband or separately. She does try to space her time so that she can be at home with her children. She is always at home on weekends, and she and her husband may entertain then.

The following story will illustrate the pace of her and her husband's life. It was told to underscore that she and her husband are partners and do things for each other.

My boy was born on Wednesday. On Saturday, Dick had an all-day meeting at our house, breakfast, lunch, and dinner; and I was in the hospital. I arranged everything from there, down to the flowers in the foyer. My doctor said I could go home, but I chose to stay [smiling] until Sunday, so I wouldn't have to be there. So what I am saying, it's not a one-way street. You have to give it back to a person. You have to want to. He is a president of a charity. I talked with him earlier [today] and he wanted to go to a function for the charity this evening. I said to him, I would really rather you go home tonight. You won't get home until eleven otherwise, and I am going to be in Florida this evening.

"Sure, if that's how you feel." It didn't matter if he was there or wasn't there, but that's how I felt.

One of Jean's priorities is to have the silver out; consequently she has someone come in every other week to clean it. A beautiful home is obviously important to her. To maintain the standards she wants, she hires extra help, as others do for different reasons.

Determining my informants' place in this spectrum of social activities and energy output is difficult unless one follows them around for a period of time. They seem not to see themselves as especially active, although they ask a lot of themselves.

Let me begin with Sandy. She gives the impression of a serene, unhurried person, although she readily acknowledges that she is a striver and is impatient with people who don't do immediately what needs to be done. Her friend Nancy's description of her seems to be accurate: "The nice thing about Sandy is that she thinks of herself as ordinary. She is, when you sit down with her. She enjoys everything she is doing at the moment, which one might not expect with someone who is doing all the things she is doing. Nothing overlaps." Nancy puts more flesh on the bones. Sandy had called her to say I would like to talk with her in connection with my research. She was not very specific about the topic. "Sandy didn't tell me what to say or what to do. 'Just talk to her.' You're on your own, so to speak." They have been close friends for over twelve years. They went to college together and have shared an apartment. Nancy saw a great deal of Sandy and Elizabeth before Richard entered the picture. Sandy and Richard's wedding was at Nancy and her husband's country house. She is a lawyer but has never practiced, is a housewife and the mother of one child. Nancy, Sandy, and two others used to have a weekly bridge club, which now has evolved into a monthly dinner meeting, minus the game. "Four very disparate people," as Nancy put it. Nancy and Sandy with their respective families also get together. The two women often talk on the telephone.

Nancy tells me some revealing stories. When Sandy comes for a weekend visit with Nancy, she refuses to sit down to relax or to sit in the sun. There must be a plan. You must do something. She can sit down in the evening with her feet up only after "she has run herself ragged for the day." Sandy has weeded Nancy's garden and cleaned out her kitchen cabinets, for example. Nancy thinks that she may be getting better about relaxing.

Nancy tells a story about Sandy's deciding one time to help Nancy with dinner, making an apple pie for dessert. She started at three in the afternoon and they ate the pie at eleven that night. She had picked the most complicated recipe. Nancy's "idea is to get dinner on the table and you are finished. Then you can sit down and enjoy the rest of the evening." But to Sandy, "There is no such thing as a simple desert." They had a great time because Sandy was chatting the whole time.

According to Nancy, Sandy reads a book once in a while but prefers to be on the go. She apparently goes to all the local fairs near the country house, perhaps because it is fun for the kids. She took Elizabeth to the local high school production of *The Sound of Music* once when Richard was in the city. There is both amusement and incredulity in Nancy's voice. She comments that she would have sat home with her daughter and a good book, relishing the fact that she didn't have anything to do.

Nancy relates how Sandy saved her on her wedding day. "Everything was going wild, everyone tripping over each other and screaming at the same time." She called Sandy, who came over right away with Elizabeth, who was an infant then. She took charge and things got organized in no time. "Everybody was happy. She always knows what people can do best. She was a godsend."

In regard to Sandy's stepchildren, Nancy volunteered:

That's another dimension to Sandy, taking over those two kids, and she really has. They really are very much a part of Sandy's life. She hasn't acquired two sort of absent children. She acquired children who take a lot of time and attention. That's Sandy, she doesn't do anything halfway.

About Sandy's mother Nancy said:

Her mother is of a different generation, but Sandy's father died when lots of those kids [her siblings] were young. She managed to pull herself together. I have a lot of admiration for her. Everybody has a thing with their mother. One of Sandy's big complaints about her mother is that she isn't organized. However, the mother still is serving Christmas and Thanksgiving dinner for twenty-five people. It makes no difference if five more come. Richard and his children were added. I really admire that very much. She is very much a mother and Sandy is also. They are alike in many ways. Sandy brings Richard's mother up to the country house a lot.

Such stories tell a good deal about Sandy's many-faceted life. Her drive and energy are enormous. Something "productive" has to be accomplished wherever she may be. One might assume that this is the pace set in the family too. As described earlier, Richard discussed Sandy's ability to accomplish so much and also his own limitation on how much he will do.

Charlene notes some of Sandy's social activities. Once a week she often has up to four guests, cooking the dinner herself. It may be friends, relatives, or business people, Charlene isn't sure. If there are more than six people, Sandy generally has the dinner catered.

Sandy told me in passing that she had had 30 members of her family up for a day to see their new country house. She frequently has lunch with family members. She reels off all their names, including their husbands, wives, and children. That's quite a few. As a matter of fact, she commented once: "Should a bomb drop on lower Manhattan, my mother would practically have her whole family wiped out." Most of them work in the Wall Street area. There is also visiting between family members in the evening, but not so frequently. Elizabeth also visits with her grandmother and apparently may stay there for many days. Sandy never told me about Elizabeth visiting by herself, but Charlene did.

Both Sandy and Richard do business entertaining at their house. They also attend parties that Richard's company gives. Sandy attends professional meetings, including the board meetings of her organization. Her stepdaughters visit at least once during the week and on weekends. Now that Sandy and Richard have a house in the city, the children will have their own rooms and may therefore spend more time with them. Sandy and Richard also have season tickets to the Philharmonic.

The same kind of drive and energy can be observed in Karin. Her social activity in a way is twofold. In her work there is a fine line between social and business friends. She has a number of work-related friends that she and her husband worked with abroad. She has many social friends, one in particular with whom she can talk over practically everything. These friends have been gathered over the years from many places, including school. Her style of entertaining is casual, except for the meals her father cooks. I understand too that a good deal is done by Andre, who is a very good cook, when they have guests. Karin does not have catered parties. She does most of the shopping herself. Her parents' alternating in staying with her and helping out is, she says, of tremendous support to her, even though they are in their seventies. I might add that she is careful not to burden her parents and is very solicitious of their welfare. She frequently goes out in the evening, taking the children and a parent along.

Karin has no family here except for her alternating parent. Her brother is in the Middle East. She is in contact with her nieces and nephew in Washington, D.C. Perhaps her having one or two friends over two to three times a week is a way of filling in for the company Andre would have provided.

Their apartment is on a high floor and therefore good for her mother's asthmatic condition, according to Karin. She cannot walk around in the streets very much because of the exhaust fumes, etc. They are looking for a new apartment which will accommodate her parents.

As noted, her mother took care of Lise when she was sick one night, changing her diapers and cleaning her. Karin, nevertheless, does not leave the children in the care of her mother alone. She always asks the housekeeper to stay when she is delayed. Nor is her father left to care for the children by himself. For one thing, he has made it clear that he wouldn't want to or know how to change diapers.

Although Karin has not lived in her native country for many years, she has many relatives there whom they see on vacation visits. She points out that her mother-in-law has always been very supportive but now lives too far away to be of any practical help.

In short, with all Karin has to do, she has not traded off social activity as a means of preserving energy and time. On the contrary, she seems to thrive on company. There is no shining silver on the table, and she may have forgotten to buy napkins. One can always use paper towels. That is the easy-going style around the house. Although she earns a sizable income, it is at present a one-income family. She cannot therefore buy additional support systems as the other women might do.

Kitty talks of how their lifestyle has changed since Bridgit was born. They don't take advantage anymore of all the things New York City has to offer, and they don't entertain the way they used to. Their friends don't get served elaborate dinners. Their lifestyle has become much more casual. Their parents think they are "crazy." She realized this especially when her in-laws came to visit over Christmas.

She thought she was in great shape, because she had bought Christmas presents several months ahead of time. They were all wrapped and ready. Her mother-in-law was horrified that she hadn't ordered and brought into the house all the food needed for the holidays. "That was the least of my worries. I can't get myself seriously upset about food arrangements." The way they entertain when in the city over weekends is having brunch with friends at their house or their friends'. "They all have children, so that is no problem." After much procrastination they had a catered business dinner, buffet style, for Peter's clients and associates. Their major business entertaining is done at lunch.

Kitty envies people with parents or in-laws just around the corner whom you can call on in emergencies. Peter's parents live far away and Kitty's parents a three-hour train ride away. "You can't get them to come on quick notice. You can't call up at 7:00 A.M. It would take too much time. Nine [times] out of ten, I could count on my mother coming down to help, if the housekeeper was going to be out for a week. So far I haven't had the need to ask." Once Peter's mother was going to come for a week to baby-sit because Kitty had a business trip to London and Peter was coming along. She decided on a two-day trip instead. Peter was surprised by how disappointed his mother had been. When their first housekeeper suddenly left, they managed with the help of housekeepers of friends and neighbors, whom Bridgit knew well. Peter's mother was coming for one week and Kitty's the following week, while they were looking for a new housekeeper. They found one so quickly that they cancelled their mothers' visits. They haven't tried any baby-sitting services yet. Kitty notes, "They check references and all that, but I have a problem with just having a stranger come in." Peter adds, "We really want to know who it is." Consequently, they have been somewhat restricted in going out without Bridgit.

My sense is that they really don't want to be away from Bridgit. They cancelled their one-week London trip. They prefer to spend all their free time with her, not going out during the week. In short, there are support systems available to them that they are reluctant to use. Whatever they do, they do together. They seem very child-focused and closeknit as a nuclear family unit.

They have extensive contact with their extended family on weekends and vacations. Their country house is a short drive from Kitty's parents. All her siblings and their families are congregated in the area. Kitty thinks they are so close because the six siblings were born within a year of one another. They see one another frequently in the country.

Kitty and Peter talk of a whole set of support systems they have at the country house. Friends, family, pediatrician, and Kitty's mother are all nearby. Her mother will help out this summer when their second child is born. According to Kitty, Peter thinks his in-laws' house rather chaotic with the number of people coming and going. The community is very child-oriented. Practically everyone has children, and Bridgit has many friends there. She stays at their houses overnight, and her friends stay at theirs. They always, however, make it a point to spend time together at the beach or go to the fair with Bridgit if the weather isn't too good.

The family spends three-day weekends at the house as often as they can as well as vacations. They are also there for Christmas and Thanksgiving holidays. It is very much a suburban lifestyle, they feel. Peter and Kitty grew up in this kind of setting. "Once we are at the house, we plan a lot of family activities, trying to make them meaningful." There is much more partying there, but it is also a much more casual life than in the city. "Are you doing anything tonight? Let's go out for dinner together"—no more formality is expected.

Kitty and Peter view their country house as their real home. "It's furnished like a regular home. We actually have nicer furniture there because we have gone to lots of auctions and we have picked up a lot of nice pieces." In their co-op they have not gotten around to getting curtains for their living room, and there are other things that need to be done. "If we don't do it before our second child is born, it will probably be a few more years before we get around to it." It can be draining to have two households, but that obviously is outweighed by the many advantages. They actually have two sets of many things, one for the city and one for the country. They have set aside one closet in the co-op where they put everything that should go to the country as they think of it. They also do most of their shopping for everything, not just food, in the country. The important thing is that they view whatever they do there as relaxation and real family time.

Catherine and George say that they have cut down their social entertaining during the week 50 to 70 percent. That was the first thing to go after Steve's birth. George has his older sons in New York City, one of whom recently became a father. He also has two nieces there. In an emergency, Steve could go to the son and daughter-in-law's, or his nieces could help out. George stresses that he would not turn to his family on a regular basis. "I am sure they would help, but they have lives of their own."

They usually have small dinners once every other week, inviting George's niece and her boyfriend or other family and friends. Catherine cooks and George cleans up. They don't do any business entertaining at home. That is generally done at lunch time.

In the country it is different. There, whoever has kids takes them along. "It's part of the scenery," comments George. Two couples in their circle of friends in the country have children the same age as Steve. The other children are older. "We generally have company Saturday evenings when we are there."

Catherine says there are times she gets "system over-loaded":

They are to some extent self-generated. Things that are discretionary. If the social calendar starts getting heavy, we can really
arrange it. Let's not go anywhere or have anyone over. Typi-
cally, stress situations can come around holiday seasons. George
is Jewish, but I was raised Catholic; and although I am not very
religious anymore, I still like a Christmas tree, bake fruitcakes,
and things like that. Last Christmas was Steve's first, kind of
an additional load in the first place. I said to myself, "Oh God,
I've really got to stop doing some things." I really was getting
short-tempered.

Initially Catherine had thought a country house would be
an added burden in an already busy life. On top of that,
theirs is over 200 years old and a restoration project. George
takes all the responsibility for this, however. "He oversees
the workmen, makes sure that things get done." Now she
is finding that the country house helps with certain things.
About an acre of their property is lawn, where they have a
sandbox for Steve, and they will be getting a jungle gym
and swing for him. Shopping is much easier there, and the
county swimming pool, where Steve can meet other children, is only a mile away. He loves the water and goes
wading in the wading pool by himself.

Catherine and George take Steve with them everywhere
in the country. "When it is cold, we try not to spend money
on heating the house. By Sunday afternoon we are kind of
tired being there and we go in the car and visit friends with
old houses on the way home." She thinks this is very good
for Steve, because he meets lots of people and is very so-
ciable, perhaps as a consequence of this.

Their house is in the best backpacking country in the East,
and they expect to go backpacking again when Steve gets
older. "George and I met backpacking." They also go on
long skiing weekends, visiting friends in Vermont. There is
a nursery there which Steve loves.

Catherine has no family in the city. Her parents live upstate. Steve stayed with his grandparents for a week once

while Catherine and George went away. Catherine had not anticipated this.

My parents are well up in their seventies. We have visited them with him several times. Once he stayed with them for two days, when he was a year old, when I had to go on a business trip. That worked out well. My mother comes out with, "When are you going to leave him for a week?" Recently, we finally did it, and he seemed very happy. They devoted their entire week to him. He didn't cry or anything. They were able to handle it. I don't know how many more years they will be able to do this. I would never ask my brothers on something like that. They have very full lives of their own and one is a grandfather. They never asked me to help out when their children were growing up.

Catherine and George hardly ever go to the movies. They have season tickets to the ballet.

Here again extended family is available to help out. They actually live nearby, so they are a good back-up system in an emergency situation. Catherine's parents have baby-sat on an extended basis in nonemergency circumstances, allowing Catherine and George to take a vacation alone.

This kind of planned help is available to Sandy and Kitty also, although Kitty has chosen not to take advantage of it.

Catherine and George don't sound as if their country house is as much of a haven of relaxation as it is for the others. The reasons for this may be many. Catherine couldn't look forward to just getting away, she had to study. Restoration of the house might take away some of the relaxation aspect. Peter too has had his share of repair work, but Kitty says that once Peter got into the swing of it, he really enjoyed it. I don't know whether Peter would agree with this assessment.

For Anna and Robert the acquiring of a country house was a compromise—a substitute for a suburban home. Robert loves to tinker and to garden. Anna likes the country but wouldn't consider commuting. She prefers the convenience of the city for work, but talks of how great the country setting is for

Michael. They do a lot of entertaining there also. Their house too is a year-round place with four bedrooms; it is an old farmhouse with a recently rebuilt kitchen with all modern conveniences. They can and frequently do have a number of people sleeping over. Robert is doing the repair work, but they also have workmen come in to paint, etc.

When I was at their apartment, Robert was talking on the telephone with weekend guests. He was the one to suggest to Anna what they would buy for dinner. He would be barbequing.

According to Anna, they have no extended family that can help out in a crisis. On the contrary, Robert often helps his parents in their business when he is free. They work so hard and such long hours that even if they wanted to baby-sit with Michael, she wouldn't let them. Her sister-in-law lives far out in the suburbs and has her own family to take care of. Anna cannot see her as helping out even in emergencies. She herself has no family in the city. Her sister and brother-in-law and their baby are studying in the United States at present. Anna is more of a resource for them than the other way around.

They celebrate both the Jewish and Christian holidays. The Jewish holidays are mostly spent at her in-laws' house and Christmas at Anna's house.

Anna does all her business entertaining at lunch; Robert has no business entertaining to do. One gets the impression that Anna keeps her work and social life very much apart. She doesn't socialize with other business people outside of work. She sticks with their old friends and the new friends she has cultivated who have children Michael's age. During the winter they entertain friends on week nights or go out with Michael in tow.

She notes that women have worked in the publishing field for a long time. She gets sufficient support and acceptance at work because of this. One day I was in her office when her boss came in to discuss her workload with her. I was invited to stay. He encouraged her to take on new responsibilities and find ways to relinquish some others that he thought less important and could be absorbed by others. Some of these she should hire a new person to do. There seems to be a less formal atmosphere in her office than the other women's offices. This, of course, may be due entirely to her boss's relaxed attitude.

I cannot calculate the amount of energy and activity that Anna has to put in, even though I followed her around. The planned time happened to be on a very slow day. Practically everyone in her office was out of town at meetings, and she was going away the next day. She could leave early. We even stopped at Bloomingdale's briefly to pick up some clothes for her trip. I went back for half a day later when everything was going at a brisk pace. People were in and out of her office constantly. I left because she had one meeting after another in the afternoon where confidential projects were going to be discussed.

Anna tackles her work and social life somewhat differently from the other women, perhaps because her husband and she are in totally unrelated fields. There is evidently less discussion of work between Anna and Robert than the others have. Even though Karin's husband is studying at present, they have common work experiences. Since Anna says that Robert doesn't really understand how it is to work in a corporation, I assume that he cannot be as helpful to Anna as the other informants' husbands appear to be when the women want to discuss their work with them. Yet she does not give the impression of being under more stress or pressure than they. This may be due to the evident sharing of responsibilities in the house and to her being in charge of its management. She keeps a delicate balance between work and family.

In summary, all my informants carried on their social activities in varying degrees after the children were born. All except Anna have extended families, and her husband perhaps participates more than the others. Being married and having children undoubtedly have something to do with my informants keeping socially active. We hear so often nowadays about the single career women with or without children who are too tired or too involved in their work to have the time to socialize. Here is another reason that the family is of such great value to the women—it is a support system which keeps them involved with the personal side of life.

The extent to which they use their extended families as support systems differs considerably. There are some ambivalent feelings about their utilization, I think. The independent "I can take care of myself" attitude is the feeling of some, others have a need to be with their children in off-work hours, some hesitate to impose on their elderly parents, and, finally, for a few of my informants extended family is not available or at least not immediately available.

The phenomenon of the country house needs special discussion. A remarkable large number of women in the success subculture that I have come across possess a weekend home. It has a profound meaning to them over and beyond what weekend houses mean to families in terms of recreation and a place to go on vacations. Some speak of it as a financial investment. Their descriptions, however, reveal the importance of the physical and emotional respite from stress that it affords. Another major ingredient is the sense of family they experience in the country house, no matter how much or how little time the family spends together in the city. Their shared life in the country is different in intensity from their city life. One gets the impression that work can't quite be shaken off in the city, even though they maintain that they can do that when they leave the office. Perhaps the proximity to the workplace impairs their freedom. At the country house work is more easily left behind. Kitty concedes that she may sometimes be in contact with the office when she is in the country. Sandy also, if she is at the house for any extended period of time, will call her secretary to check on how things are going. The various reasons for this contact—stimulation, keeping on top of job—have been discussed earlier.

Most view the house as a compromise with living in the suburbs. Their apartments in the city are obviously convenient in the short travel to work. Their country houses range in distance from about 75 to 150 miles from their apartments. Their homes in the city are work-related; there they lay their bodies down to sleep. On the whole there is nothing extraordinary about their apartments. They are not illustrations from *House Beautiful* or *Town and Country* magazines; they are functional and comfortable. The country houses may be different. Catherine and George's is over 200 years old. Kitty mentions that they have better furniture there.

My informants' comments indicate that an hour or so out of the city they begin to shed their work and concentrate on their family lives. They speak of those houses as more like real homes than their city dwellings. Actually, all my informants' houses are year-round homes where they go in all seasons. Many spend Christmas and Thanksgiving there. They report enjoying being snowed in.

A great deal of time is spent repairing and restoring the houses. The lawn mowing, the gardening, all have the familiar ring of the suburbanite talking. Here they entertain in a casual way, they say.

In short, despite extra work, the country house is a major support system. One obviously can do without it, but it eases their lives and brings them a sense of well-being. It gives an outlet, a relief from work, a kind of rejuvenation, and a time to focus on their family life. It is concentrated time and, I guess it could be called quality time. It is the family affair!

8

Summary

The women of the success subculture fly in the face of many a myth about how women should feel, live, and behave. In that sense they are iconoclasts. Not that they necessarily set out to be, but living on the cutting edge of a changing society almost inevitably makes them so. They have entered paths few women have trod—the high-echelon, prestigious, and well-paid jobs near the top of the organizational and social hierarchy. They live in relatively egalitarian marriages and are mothers as well. They upset traditional views of marriage where the husband is the major earner "entitled" to privilege. Perhaps most disturbing to many of their critics is their challenge to the sacredness of motherhood, i.e., to the belief that child rearing is the mother's first responsibility, and hers alone.

It is not surprising, therefore, that these women are viewed with such strong and mixed feelings: awe and admiration by some, envy or severe criticism by others. All the more reason, then, to study them through the ethnographic method, which attempts to avoid one's own biases and to learn about the success subculture and its inhabitants from their point of view. Learning about a subculture and the people who live in it does not mean that one must know a large number of people well. I chose five women —an arbitrary number— to get a small spectrum of the functioning of successful career women. The informants were preselected to fit the criteria: being in a high-echelon job, usually occupied by men; earning over $50,000; having a young child; and living in New York City. They range in age from 32 to 37.

These women, who have climbed close to the top in management and who are also married and mothers, refute the contention of male top management in business and the professions that marital obligations prevent married women from making it to the top. The reason that they are not found there obviously lies elsewhere.

"Anyone can make it to where I am if you work hard and don't set roadblocks in your way" is a myth many of the women themselves cherish and are loath to relinquish. To accept that they have help along the way—a "sustaining crowd" of family, friends, colleagues, professional groups, mentors, housekeepers, secretaries, and a wide variety of dependable helpers—is perhaps an affront to the ego and to their belief in individualism. Most of the women invariably contradict themselves on this point by giving recognition to their sustaining crowd. Having help along the way certainly does not negate their personal input and their hard work. As we have seen throughout this book, it takes many people and circumstances to make one successful career, be it a man's or a woman's. But women in general have fewer opportunities and more obstacles placed in their way to the top than their male counterparts. Men have always had "the old boys' network" to help them in moving up the ladder.

A look at the backgrounds of the women in the study, noting the times they were born into—one in which greater opportunities opened up for women—their socialization process, their personalities, their intelligence, education, mentors, the color of their skin, even their attractiveness, makes it clear that all these components interacted to enable them to enter the opportunity structure of their hierarchy. Once in this structure their chances for increasing their opportunities and power grow, as Kanter (1982:247) suggests. They are on the fast track.

The women in the success subculture expect of themselves and of each other adherence to certain rules and values, frequently unspoken. They are unswervingly committed to their careers. Many get their MBAs and other degrees by going to school at night. They are extremely self-confident, highly goal-oriented, hardworking, and energetic. They have a very optimistic approach to life. Complaining, they feel, is unproductive; either things are judged important and made priorities, or they are delegated or dropped. The women role model for each other. Advice and support are freely given to women who keep to these rules and values. They are less tolerant of those who do not.

They consistently behave in ways that they think will "not place roadblocks" in their way to upward mobility. For example, they may work until the day a baby is born or take very short maternity leaves, whether they like it or not. Until recently they kept quiet about their motherhood. They ignore overt sexism whenever possible, but if it stands in their way, they will tackle it or find a way around it. Competition is fierce. Jean (pilot study), who is extremely career focused, more so than my informants, describes the competition well: "Superwoman? Only if you are on the outside. If inside, you are being matched hour by the hour by men on the right and women on the left. . . . It's like flying with the rest." In essence Jean is saying that women have to work according to the rules of the game, structured by and for men, if they want to be in the race.

Most successful career women agree that it is important to establish themselves in their careers before they have children and that having children slows them down temporarily. Their career progression from then on depends on how career focused they are. They have the option of slowing down if they decide the personal cost is too high. Catherine comments, for example, "I love my career and I'm

happy, but I am also not going to work twelve hours a day."
This, of course, does not mean that they can sit back and
relax. They have to keep up with the demands of the job,
the pace is fast, and their performance has to be above
average. The successful women function very similarly to
their successful male colleagues, except for the importance
the women place on their family role.

Those women who want to get back into the race seriously
soon after children are born need to give up family time.
They run the gauntlet; the double standard for women and
men seems to become even more pronounced for them. The
women themselves believe there is no other way to break
into the power structure of the senior-echelon positions reserved for men except on the men's terms. Even so, many
of the women do not think it possible to reach the top until
the present generation of senior executives retires in ten to
fifteen years. The extent to which the women emphasize
their family role is highly idiosyncratic, depending on how
fast and how far the individual woman wants to move in
her career.

The successful career women also challenge tradition in requiring partnership with their husbands. Their wish and need
for intimate relationships is clear. They can demand partnership because they are financially independent of their husbands and share more or less equally with them in the family's
expenses. They contribute substantially to the family's high
standards of living, to its status and prestige. Women who
are economically dependent to varying degrees on their husbands have less leverage for such a demand. Model (1982)
and her associates found in a study of husband participation
in household tasks that the less differential in income between
spouses, the more the husbands participated. In the success
subculture the traditional dominant-subordinate structure of
marriage shifts to a more egalitarian one.

My informants' husbands, who are successful in their own
right, accept their wives as career women, respect and ad-

mire their achievements, and support them in their careers. For example, one husband collects clippings from the newspapers in which his wife is quoted to show friends and pushes her to get an advanced degree, even though it means she has to study two evenings a week and on Saturday mornings. Their acceptance, I believe, is a prerequisite for these marriages to work. Despite the husbands' traditional upbringing, they have learned to participate in household chores and child care although their wives have the overall burden of the responsibility.

It is in regard to husband participation or the lack of it that the women in the success subculture raise the most questions in the women's organization meetings. "We both think we do 75 percent of the work," some remark. "Husbands are trainable," the women say. Stories of how they teach husbands about cleaning bathrooms, sorting laundry, etc., illustrate this strategy. The women also deliberately leave household tasks undone for their husbands to do without asking their help. You hear comments like these: "We're just asking for it when we say 'Gee, will you help me out?' I don't buy that at all." "It is not my house. It's our house. It is not mother's work. It's parents' work." Another strategy which requires the aquiescence of husbands is lowering the standards for house-cleaning and meal-making. As we have seen, my informants' husbands participate a great deal in the care of children; some cook, do shopping, laundry, and cleaning when the housekeeper is not around. They are important support both practically and emotionally to their wives, as the women are to their husbands.

Yet my informants draw a line beyond which they do not expect their husbands to participate. They apparently feel their own responsibility for the management of child care and household is balanced by other things that their husbands do and by the considerable, sometimes the major influence they have in decision-making. In accepting the management role they do fall into a traditional role for women.

They have not really stopped to question it, as they have so many other things. "Somebody has to fill the void," says Kitty, although otherwise she is one of the staunchest advocates of leaving things for the husbands to do. There is a delicate balance of power in these interdependent relationships. However, until their husbands share in the management of child care and household, their marriages are not truly egalitarian. The couples seem to feel that the satisfaction they derive from the present arrangement outweighs the chores and responsibilities each of them assumes. These families are all close-knit.

Public opinion seriously questions whether working women can be "good" mothers, as revealed in the 1982 survey of working Americans described in chapter 5 (Kagan 1983). A majority even feel women should not have children at all if they plan to stay in the labor market. Thus people's beliefs lag far behind the reality in today's America where the majority of married women are in the work force and the number is steadily increasing. The number of married women in paid employment with children under the age of 6 jumped from 16.6 percent in 1960 to 48.7 percent in 1982 (U.S. Bureau of the Census 1984). These trends are continuing because women need to work out of economic necessity, if for no other reason. The women in the success subculture work because they want to. They challenge the stereotypical notion that motherhood is an all-encompassing, all-fulfilling occupation for *all* women. This myth was exploded by Friedan in *the Femine Mystique* and by others in the women's movement in the 1960s, but it still lingers. Baruch, Barnett, and Rivers (1983:88-93) in their study of approximately 300 women found that motherhood can be one of the greatest sources of stress. Their findings underscore the fallacy of making one blueprint fit all women.

The women in the success subculture make it emphatically clear that they can not conceive of staying home and taking care of their children exculsively. Many freely admit that their patience wears thin when they are confined to the home. Others who wanted to stay home longer did not for fear that they would not be viewed as serious about their careers. To fulfill themselves, they want and need their careers. They also have a sense that they can give more to their children because of the stimulation they derive from their work. Many of them told me that often when they return home from work their steps quicken in anticipation of spending time with their children. They believe they can organize their social systems better when they work. They don't feel they have to do everything around the house; they can say no to excessive demands. Baruch, Barnett, and Rivers (1983) corroborate these findings.

Nevertheless, child care is the one area in which the women in the success subculture appear to feel vulnerable. The reason is partly, I think, that they cannot control their children's development as they believe they can their careers. They do want to be in charge of their lives, and here is an uncertainty that they cannot fully master. Partly, perhaps, some guilt is engendered by their own socialization process in which their mothers stayed home with them until they were at least of school age. They try to insulate themselves from criticism by surrounding themselves with people whose lives are like theirs. That they cannot entirely escape criticism was evident by the stories they told at the Working Mothers' luncheons about people who disapprove of their lifestyle.

The children are clearly an extremely important part of my informants' lives, as their detailed descriptions of their involvement with them, the stories they tell, and my observations all show. The women are ingenious in finding ways to spend time with their children. They will take time whenever possible to visit the children's schools for an important event, go with them to pediatricians, and deal with emergencies, making up time later. This flexibility is possible because of their privileged positions in the organizational hierarchy.

They try to balance their time between the children and their jobs. The latter must of necessity come first. The children are looked after by trusted caretakers. They have to adjust to their mothers' work patterns. The mothers have managed to limit their working hours to a great extent, at least while the children are young. They can do this mainly because they have already established themselves in their careers. People know them and know that the work will get done.

My informants clearly take their mothering seriously. Karin believes she spends as much time with her children as does a mother who stays at home. Despite arduous schedules during the day, Karin gets up to feed the baby several times at night. Sandy, even though she has a housekeeper available, tends to her daughter during the night when such care is needed.

The women are not denying their wish to nurture, nor their children's need of nurturing. They are simply challenging the notions that motherhood alone should fill their lives and that the caring for the child should be done by them alone. Their ability to afford good child care minimizes whatever guilt they might experience.

Here perhaps is where these women differ most obviously from the majority of working women. Our national policy toward child care is in drastic need of improvement. The reality that mothers of young children in increasing numbers have to work makes good day care facilities a desperate priority. The scandals that echo across the country regarding sexual abuse of children and substandard conditions in many such centers point to a lack of public and political concern that does not make life easier for the mothers who cannot afford good caretakers in the home or elsewhere. Only when the standards in child care facilities are raised and the numbers of such facilities approach adequacy, will there be less cause for uneasiness by working mothers on a widespread basis. At this time the patriarchal system is still at play, making change very difficult, trapping women and children in a system that requires the women to work out of financial need, if for no other reason, but does little if anything to help arrange for the care of the children. The myth that everyone can work themselves to a level of affluence—a myth many of these women believe—has been exploded many times over. If excellent child care resources were extensively available, public opinion toward mothers' right to work outside the home would undoubtedly become more accepting.

For many years Chess and Thomas have advocated shifting the emphasis from who is doing the nurturing to the child's need for nurturing. This opens the door for fathers to become involved, allowing them to experience closeness with their children and partake in their development. My informants' husbands express pleasure in both words and actions in this kind of involvement, which has become a familiar pattern for many fathers today. There are many attitudinal and structural changes that need to be made in the workplace to realize such involvement, such as introducing paternity leaves on a widespread basis. The future holds many unknowns when it comes to the effect the fathers' new intimacy with their children will have; their socialization processes will be different. If the trend of fathers' greater involvement continues, no doubt child rearing theories will need to be revised.

The housekeeper or nursemaid, as the case may be, also has, of course, an effect on the children in the success subculture. To my knowledge little research has been done in the United States on her impact on these children. She is their caretaker when their parents are not around. This is her primary function—to be available whenever needed. If she is not, other help has to be hired. Her presence relieves the career women of much of the complicated planning less affluent women have to work out around child care. The standards set for her other responsibilities, such as house cleaning, laundry, etc., are secondary. Nevertheless, she obviously creates comfort for the career women and their families by keeping the home in relatively good shape. Heavy cleaning help is also brought in.

The housekeeper is the mainstay of the woman's successful functioning—her number one support system. She is frequently a "green card lady" (a legal alien with a work permit), who generally comes from the West Indies. The nursemaids are usually from England, Scotland, or Ireland. The nursemaids are more established, more professional in their concept of themselves, and therefore not so emotionally involved nor so flexible in their working hours as the "green card ladies." Many of the West Indians are in the process of establishing themselves in this country, often with families still at home.

The children's caretaker needs to be fully trusted by her employer. The career women go to great lengths to ensure her well-being. Often a caring, interdependent relationship develops between the "green card lady" and the career women. Most of the women prefer a live-out housekeeper to ensure their own privacy to some extent, but those who have irregular working hours or travel a great deal need a live-in housekeeper. The housekeeper is, figuratively speaking, often as much of a slave to her employer's work as the career women themselves are. In other words, she functions to some extent like a wife in the traditional family.

Sociologists emphasize that the career women themselves are escaping "some of the constraints of sex stratification" at the expense of a class of women who are the most limited by it and that this creates very little change in the traditional domestic division of labor (Hunt and Hunt 1982b:44). This ironic fact reverts to the belief that many of the successful women hold that anyone can make it to their level, that everyone has equal opportunities. Suffice it to say here that my informants themselves were the recipients of expanded opportunities for women. They do try on an individual basis to help those housekeepers who are interested to improve themselves socioeconomically; they become mentors.

There are, of course, numerous other support systems in the successful career women's lives. Two major ones are their extended families and friends, and their weekend houses. Despite the cutting down on their social life when the children are born, they do keep up with their friends and their families. Most of my informants' extended families for one reason or another are not available as back-up systems in emergencies, but most of them can arrange babysitting with advance planning. There is extensive contact with extended families. Friends are also around. In short, my informants and their families are not isolated nuclear families but are fully involved with relatives and friends who for the most part support their lifestyles. A great many of the women I met during my research and most of my informants have country houses where they go as often as possible to spend time together as a family, to socialize, and to get away from the pressures of work. Despite the extra work these houses involve, they are a real safety valve.

Career, marriage, children, household, and social life are all part of social life systems which have to be managed and coordinated. I view the career women as general managers of these social systems. In addition to the personality attributes described earlier, they need to be bright and personable, to like to influence people, to enjoy organized work, and to possess managerial skills in order to perform well in such complex systems. Their first priority is to free time to devote to their careers. Their secretaries, especially, are important in minimizing the encroachment of personal and family responsibilities on the job. The women at times accomplish this through the use of their secretaries in personal matters, not unlike the "traditional" way men use their secretaries, though the tasks may be dissimilar. They generally rationalize this by rewarding the secretaries in a variety of ways, such as giving them more power, higher pay, personal attention, and favors. Husbands frequently may be involved as babysitters, cooks, shoppers, etc. The housekeepers are in charge of the children; they and the cleaning women take care of the house and the laundry. Extended family, weekend houses, friends, babysitters, caterers, cleaners, restaurants that deliver ready-to-eat food are just samples of the support systems available to these families. The women themselves, however, must coordinate.

A discernible pattern of management emerges from an examination of the functioning of the women who are successful in handling their several roles without getting frazzled. The key is their effective use of the sustaining crowd. The strategies these women use are to plan, to delegate tasks and responsibilities and give careful instructions regarding them, and to surround themselves with competent people whom they can trust and use to do the work they cannot or do not want to do themselves. The tasks and responsibilities differ with each woman. The less bound by conventions and guilt the women are, the freer they are to delegate and in turn the freer to pursue what they want to do. Lowering of standards is an important strategy. The women who need to cook a great meal every day are in trouble. Another skill is compartmentalization, focusing on one thing at a time, tuning out other areas of their lives. This prevents one role from interfering with another. They need to establish adequate reward systems for everyone concerned, including themselves. Professional organizations and networks provide tangible and emotional support and spur them on to do more.

The higher the standards set, the more tasks the women must delegate; the less husband participation in the household, the more support systems have to be hired. This is the basic rule that makes the social system run smoothly. It is clearly a complex management task requiring not only managerial skills but energy—a crucial element that the women appear to have in abundance.

Where the women in the success subculture get their energy is a puzzlement to many and was to me at the beginning of my research. Listening to and observing their upbeat approach to life led me to conclude that the solution to the puzzle lies in their high commitment to their careers, children, and marriages. The pleasure they obtain in these various roles energizes them to go for more. It is a beneficial circle—the exact opposite of a vicious one.

The conventional expectation that our energy will be drained by each activity we undertake does not hold true for all, and my informants are excellent examples. Marks (1977) suggests an energy-creation theory of multiple roles when energy is created by the satisfaction of and the rewards for a job well done. He believes that we find energy "for anything to which we are highly committed and we often feel more energetic after having done it." Doing something we are not committed to on the other hand, often leaves us feeling tired (1977:926–27). Thus Marks, and also Sieber (1974), support my conclusion, and elucidate Baruch, Barnett, and Rivers' (1983:43) findings that married women with children in high-echelon jobs were rated the highest on all their indices of well-being.

At the time of my research, all my informants were balancing their family roles fairly equitably with their careers, suggesting that realizing themselves and being intimately connected with others are not mutually exclusive. Doing both can be a freeing experience for women as well as those with whom they are affiliated (Miller 1976:116). My informants' certainty of their rights to realize themselves through their career achievements frees them of much of the guilt other women carry around for relinquishing traditional sex-role expectations. Their husbands, although giving up much power in the relationships with their wives, are free from their wives' complete dependency on them financially and emotionally. They are free to become more emotionally in-volved with their children—not like the fathers of the past whose undisputed role of power as head-of-household kept them apart.

Similarly, my informants' interaction with the people around them supports Gilligan's (1982:173) findings which suggest that women through their psychological developmental process are generally more interconnected, caring, and re-sponsible in their relationships than are most men. This does not deny, of course, that many men have similar qualities and that many women may lack some of them. My inform-ants demonstrate their need for intimate affiliation in their wish for husbands and children. They are autonomous, yet interconnected.

The changes in the psychological perception of women have been slow in evolving. This trend underscores my sense that socioeconomic, cultural, and political forces greatly influence psychological theories as a whole, and vice versa. The classic psychoanalytic theory, as it has been traditionally interpreted in the United States, contributed to the status quo of women's subordination and the patriarchy. It became so widely popularized in America, I believe, because it served the cause of the male hierarchy and their individualism so well. These are not new ideas, by any means. Friedan and others have expounded them since the sixties, and many women and men before them.

New psychological theories, ideas, and fads are constantly forthcoming to cope with the problems of human beings in the technological age. Medicine is discovering things about the brain that might outdate as well as contribute a great deal to our beliefs about human behavior. However, human behavior has to be in accord with the culture and its rules for people to belong. The power structure tends to deter-mine change. The question then, is whether women like those discussed in this book exist in sufficient numbers, and whether they are willing, to press for more humanity and interconnection in relationships with others. Will their more egalitarian relationships with men make a big enough dent? Will enough men be willing to be deviant and join women in order to share in intimacy? The women can only succeed from a position of power—that is, shared power with men. Will they still care enough once in power? Will they even get there? These are questions only the future can answer. But there seems to be hope when one looks at what is happening in the families described in this book.

The women in this subculture are not "superwomen," as the media so often proclaim them to be. To view them so seems to me to be tantamount to saying that only superwomen have the ability to function on an equal level with successful men. The women are meeting the requirements of the demanding job of a general manager and are therefore, obviously, not run-of-the-mill people, but neither are their male counterparts. Their way of life is of their own choice—and indeed they have choices. Each is unique, but their stories are the social construction of success.

Appendix

One Morning at Anna's Office

My second visit to Anna's office. The first time was an unusually quiet day because most of her colleagues were away at meetings. This time it is a typical day, according to Anna. Her office is on the seventeenth floor. It is medium-sized and modern with a large desk and a beautiful view. When Anna is on the telephone, she swivels her chair around and looks out. There are three comfortable chairs with armrests in her office. A large tree makes up the decoration. A computer locked into the company's "nerve center" is on a low cabinet. Walls are bare; a picture of Michael is on another cabinet. It is a very orderly office, everything neatly stacked in racks.

9:20 A.M.   Anna and I arrive almost simultaneously. Call is waiting for her.

9:30   Her secretary comes in with urgent messages. (Anna has been out of town for a couple of days.) Anna sorts her mail, arranging it on the desk according to importance. She starts going through the mail.

9:50   Incoming business call. Brief. She continues to look at mail.

10:00   Leaves office.

10:01   Secretary comes in with folder.

10:04   Anna is back. Calls secretary.

10:05	Incoming brief call.
10:07	Colleague in hurry stops by to say hello. (Anna's door is always open.)
10:09	Incoming business call.
10:26	Anna introduces me to a colleague; several other people stop by. She finishes reading her mail and jots down some responses.
10:50	Her boss comes in. Brief discussion. He leaves.
11:03	Incoming call. She discusses code name project.
11:05	Another director comes in. I leave because code name project is to be discussed.
11:15	Meeting finished.
11:16	Incoming call from Ivy League university. Would she lead a seminar? Her name has been suggested to them by ex-boss. Good publicity, but she doesn't think she has the time. Will suggest someone else.
11:24	Anna has started on a report, using calculator for figures. She is preparing for the various afternoon meetings.
11:35	Her boss comes in to discuss her workload. He wants her to take on new responsibilities, important tasks, and hire someone to pick up things she needs to delegate.
12:06 P.M.	Boss leaves.
12:07	Anna leaves briefly to talk with secretary.
12:09	Goes to check if colleague can have lunch with her to discuss secret project. Returns shortly. Tells secretary to make lunch reservations. In afternoon has meetings one after the other which all involve secret projects. Anna continues doing desk work.
12:30	I leave.

Day Spent with Anna

7:48 A.M.   I arrive at apartment. Anna, in dressing gown, is drinking coffee and reading the *New York Times* in dining alcove. Michael is sitting in highchair eating cereal and watching a children's program on TV nearby.

7:50   Michael wants to show me his room. He is not finished with his cereal, but gets down. His room has his bed and a sofa bed and is crammed with toys. Gay pictures hang on the wall.

7:55   Mary arrives. Michael has put on his tape recorder and is playing his favorite song.

8:00   Anna comes in to explain she is always late for office. She usually leaves at 8:45. It takes her 25 minutes door to door. She goes back to dining room to finish paper and breakfast.

8:05   Robert comes in dressed in casual clothing. After introducing himself, he tells me he is going to his parents' business to help out because he has the day off from work. He talks with Michael for a few minutes and gets their day's program from Mary. He leaves, saying he is late.

8:15   Anna leaves table and goes to get dressed. I talk with Mary and Michael.

8:45   Anna is ready. She tells Mary to take something to the cleaners. Cleaning woman is coming that day. Anna has left money on the counter for her.

8:50   We leave. Michael is at the door saying goodbye. Anna stops at the cleaners to make certain clothes are ready for her trip to attend company seminar in the South for three days. She stops at the bank for money. Anna warns me several times that this is a bad day to visit her office because practically everyone is out of town and it will be very quiet. We walk to subway.

9:30	We arrive at her office. I am introduced to her secretary, whom Anna praises highly. Later I speak with the secretary at length.

The day was indeed quiet, I am therefore skipping the details. Anna states she gets more tired when it is slow than when it is really busy. She tells me a great deal about her work, which sounds extremely interesting. She is in a very important position in her company, involving a lot of research and planning on her part. She recommends and has a lot of input in projects that can mean great financial profit for her company and also the reverse. We went to a business luncheon with a colleague from the Coast who was five months pregnant and an associate of hers. Anna is clearly the authority and they are trying to sell her their ideas.

5:15 P.M.	Robert calls to tell Anna what he has picked up for dinner. Anna says, she will pick up salad ingredients. She asks if he has bought cheese, which he has.
5:20	Anna decides to leave and finish what she is working on the next day, which also will be slow.
5:25	Subway to Bloomingdale's. Anna wants to pick up sport shirts for her trip to the South.
6:10	From there we take bus to her house.
6:20	Anna buys vegetables at greengrocer's near her house.
6:30	We arrive at her apartment. Michael greets us at the door. He is in his pajamas and wants to know what Anna has brought him. She tells me they often bring him something. Robert has bought him a book that day. Robert is reading in the living room.
6:40	We eat cheese that Robert has put out. Anna talks with Michael.
6:50	Anna goes to change. Robert serves drinks and we talk.

7:00   Anna returns and eats some more cheese while con-
        tinuing to talk with Michael.

7:10   She and Michael start dinner. He helps wash the
        vegetables.

7:15   She and Michael set the table after asking Robert
        several times to do this. He facetiously replies he
        is busy being interviewed. He has put the water on
        for the pasta. Michael has already eaten. Michael
        comes in, wants our attention. Robert talks with
        him and proudly tells me about his various accom-
        plishments.

7:35   We sit down to eat the pasta with sauce Robert has
        bought in a pasta place. There is cheese, bread, and
        butter. Michael sits with us for a while. Then turns
        on his tape recorder nearby. He returns for dessert
        (ice cream). Robert entertains us with his experiences
        at his parents' business that day. We talk until 8:30.
        Telephone call from a forthcoming weekend guest
        during dinner, which Robert takes. When he returns,
        he suggests to Anna what he will buy to barbecue
        over the weekend.

8:30   Robert starts clearing the table and Anna puts the
        dishes in the dishwasher. Michael and I go to the
        living room.

8:40   Anna comes in. She tells me more about her job
        history. Michael wants more attention from her. She
        quiets him down. I notice Robert taking the garbage
        out in the background. When he comes back, he
        divides his time reading his new book on gardening
        and talking with Michael. Now and then he partici-
        pates in our conversation. Anna talks about their
        friends, involving Robert at times. She shows me
        pictures of their new country house, and they all talk
        about their life there. They clearly enjoy the place
        tremendously. Robert talks about the work he is doing
        there. They discuss plans for the house.

9:00   Anna starts taking out glasses and carafes to bring
            to the country, checking with Robert what he thinks
            they should bring. Robert tells me how to make plants
            grow as beautiful as theirs. He takes care of them.

9:30   Michael is still up. Apparently he takes a nap during
            the day. I leave.

Karin's Own Log of Activities

Monday, April 11th
Hour   *Activity*

3:00–3:20 A.M.
                          Nursing.

5:00–5:15   Nursing.

7:00–8:30   Get up, make breakfast, change Marcel and
                          Lise, give instructions on dinner to mother,
                          collect notes on apartments, talk to Barbara.

8:30–9:00   Transit.

9:00–10:10   Medical checkup. Doctor says I should take
                          better care of myself, rest, and exercise. (!)

10:10–11:50   Work. Make 3 calls for apartments. Call to
                          Barbara to arrange for her to stay late so I can
                          go see an apartment.

11:50–1:30 P.M.   Working luncheon.

1:30–2:15   Bank to get quarters for washing clothes, look
                          at bulletin boards for apartments.

2:15–4:45   Work.

4:45–6:30   Look at apartment.

6:30–6:45   Nursing.

6:45–7:00   Dinner (Mother prepares).

7:00–7:15   Nursing.

7:15–9:15   Play with Lise, walking and running up and
                          down stairs and corridor, carrying Marcel un-
                          til he goes to bed 8:30, Lise bath 7:30–8:00.

9:15–10:30   Work (papers to read) and sort out medical
                          insurance papers.

10:30–11:00   Feed Marcel (bottle), change diaper.

Tuesday, April 12th

2:30–2:45 A.M.	Nursing.
4:30	Marcel woke up, nursed him—he did not want to go to sleep again.
7:00–8:20	Out of bed, prepare breakfast, change and clean both children, eat, read *New York Times*, arrange for Barbara stay late.
8:50–12:30 P.M.	Work. Phone calls to determine procedures for citizenship application, dependency allowance.
12:30–1:15	Lunch with colleague who has child care center, visit center.
1:15–5:30	Work.
5:30–6:30	Look at apartment.
6:30–6:45	Nursing.
6:45–7:15	Dinner. 15 minutes for phone call to Andre.
8:00–8:15	Nursing.
7:15–9:15	Play with Lise; Marcel to bed 8:15.
9:15–10:00	Read newspapers.
10:00–10:15	Nurse Marcel, prepare bottle for tonight.
10:15	Bed.

Wednesday, April 13th

3:00–3:20 A.M.	Bottle feed, change Marcel.
5:00–5:15	Nurse. Several times 5:15–8:00 Marcel wakes, and I tell him to go back to sleep.
8:00–8:30	Get up because Lise wakes me. Breakfast etc.
8:30	Off to work.

9:00–5:30 P.M.	Worked straight through, a few calls re apartments, also tried unsuccessfully call nursery school, 15 minutes for lunch.
5:30–6:00	Transit.
6:00	Eat (feed Marcel 20 minutes).
6:30	Bathe Lise, dress her in sleep wear.
7:10	Play with both children.
7:30	"Muppet" show (TV).
8:00	Put Marcel to bed.
8:10–9:00	Read with Lise, run in corridor, throw garbage out.
9:00–10:00	Phone calls, read paper, read a paper for work.
10:00	Bed—no time for bath.

Day Spent with Karin

7:45 A.M.	I arrive. Karin at door with Marcel in her arms. Lise comes in, looking a bit under the weather. She has a pacifier. It's the first time in a month she has wanted this, explains Karin. She has been sick during the night. Karin is mad at a friend who brought her child over who had a cold. Karin is obviously concerned. Her mother comes in in her dressing gown. Everyone eats breakfast, cereal, toast, jam, and cheese. Karin tells me Marcel woke up for feeding at 4:40 A.M. and then at 6:00 A.M. Karin is speaking three languages simultaneously, one to the kids, one to her mother, and another to me.
8:15	Barbara arrives. Marcel is drooling all over Karin. Lise wants to sit on her lap and then plays with Marcel. Karin goes to change, while Barbara changes Marcel. Barbara leaves Marcel unattended on top of the dressing table when she hears Lise crying. Karin notices and goes in. She doesn't comment until we are on our way home. She remarks almost to herself, "I have never seen Barbara do anything like that before. She must have been upset about Lise crying."
8:30	We leave for work. Lise comes with us to the elevator. She doesn't cry when we leave. Barbara brings her back to the apartment. Karin walks at high speed to the subway station. We have to make one transfer. At the station, Karin takes out her calendar to see what lies ahead. She always does that at home, she says, but was too preoccupied with what was going on.
9:00	We arrive at her office. All the offices are relatively small. Karin's office is decorated with

a large plant, a map with flags on the wall, a bulletin board. Lise's art work hangs on it. There are a couple of calendars hanging on the wall which show vacation times and conferences, etc. The office furniture is regular gray metal. Everything is strictly functional, except for the plants. The receptionist outside her office tells her they are trying urgently to reach her boss who is en route someplace far away. Messages have been left everywhere.

9:05	Karin starts working at her desk.
9:20	A male subordinate comes in with papers. Her boss calls. He gets his messages from the receptionist. Karin goes out to talk with him. Returns.
9:35	Karin leaves office.
9:40	She returns with female Financial Assistant to show her something.
9:43	Karin goes to talk with receptionist. (Again she is continually switching languages. Everyone appears to be of a different nationality.)
9:48	Karin asks if it is OK with me if she goes on short business visits around the office without my tagging along. It will take too much time otherwise. She leaves.
9:50	She comes back with staff member, who sits next to Karin's desk discussing business.
10:10	They both leave office.
10:25	Both return, finish their business, and he leaves.
10:30	Karin leaves with papers.

10:32	She returns, reads papers at her desk. She leaves a couple of more times with papers and returns.
10:40	Her secretary comes in. They work on staff schedules and go over budgets for various people and offices.
10:47	Staff member returns, but withdraws when he sees secretary at her desk. Karin gets call. He finally ventures in, puts papers on her desk, stands waiting. As Karin is talking on the phone, she uses papers he has brought in. She interrupts conversation and asks him if he has seen a contract. They are talking about some employee contract. Secretary remains seated.
11:00	Staff member leaves. Secretary takes dictation. They go over budget. Secretary has to make out new schedules for expenditures.
11:25	Secretary leaves.
11:27	Karin leaves.
11:35	Woman comes in with folder, puts it on Karin's desk, and leaves.
11:40	Secretary brings in message and leaves it on desk.
11:42	Karin returns. Goes through mail, remarks, she is on all the sucker lists. She sends money to anything that has to do with women's rights, nuclear issues, and Amnesty International.
11:50	Karin calls someone to ask him/her to attend a conference. She apparently doesn't have to do this for the time being. (It means traveling.)

12:01 P.M.	Talks to receptionist to get call through to distant country.
12:05	Karin works at desk, puts on shawl. Air conditioning makes office freezing. Her cold is getting worse. She says, since her stay in the Far East, the cold never seems to quite go away.
12:15	Karin leaves.
12:20	She calls real estate agents about apartments. Leaves messages.
12:28	We go out in search of batteries for her watch. Fast pace. We eat quick lunch at lunch counter.
1:55	We return to office.
	Same busy schedule continues until 5:25 P.M.
5:25	Karin takes out of a bunch of reports she has received earlier, what she will need to work on at home. She has to have some tables ready for tomorrow. She hasn't been able to finish them at the office. She could stay and work, but says she has to be careful with money and it costs a lot to pay Barbara overtime. Karin has forgotten to tell her mother that I am coming home with her, so I stop off to buy some dinner.
6:25	I arrive at their apartment. They are all finishing dinner. Mother has cooked, clears the table, and takes care of the dishes.
6:45	Karin plays with Lise on the terrace while holding Marcel in one arm.
7:00	Karin draws bath for Lise and helps her undress, mostly by suggesting to Lise what to take off next, helping her when it becomes too difficult.

7:10	Lise gets into tub. Marcel has already been bathed by Barbara. Karin directs Lise how to wash herself while holding Marcel. She gives Lise her toothbrush while she demonstrates to her how to do it by brushing her own teeth and still holding Marcel. Quite a balancing act. She briefly gives Marcel to her mother while she finishes washing Lise and gets her into her pajamas.
7:30	Everyone watches the "Muppet" show on TV. Lise sits next to her mother. Marcel sits in a large chair, being watched closely, in case he should need rescue. When Marcel starts crying, Karin puts him on her lap. Lise plays with her toys when the show is finished.
8:10	Karin puts Marcel in crib in his room, then takes Lise to bed and reads her a story.
8:30	Both come back again. Lise is not sleepy. She plays some more.
8:40	Marcel starts to cry. Karin picks him up, rocks him.
8:50	Marcel is put back to bed again.
9:00	Lise now wants to go to bed. Karin takes her.
9:10	Everything seems quiet finally. I leave. Karin is going to finish the tables for tomorrow's deadline. First time, she says, she has done this kind of work at home since the kids were born. Reading for work, she doesn't consider real work.

Bibliography

Adams, Carolyn Teich and Cathryn Teich Winston. 1980. *Mothers at Work: Public Policies in the United States, Sweden, and China*. New York: Longman.

Aldous, Joan. 1982, ed. *Two Paychecks: Life in Dual-Career Families*. Beverly Hills: Sage.

Appelbaum, Eileen. 1981. *Back to Work: Determinants of Women's Successful Re-entry*. Boston: Auburn House.

Barnett, Rosalind C. and Grace K. Baruch. 1978. *The Competent Woman: Perspectives on Development*. New York: Halsted Press.

Baruch, Grace, Rosalind Barnett, and Caryl Rivers. 1983. *Lifeprints: New Patterns of Love and Work for Today's Women*. New York: New American Library.

Beardsley, Elizabeth Lane. 1982. "On Curing Conceptual Confusion: Response to Mary Ann Warren." In Mary Vetterling-Braggin, ed., *"Femininity," "Masculinity," and "Androgyny,"* pp. 197–200. Totowa, N.J.: Littlefield, Adams.

Bernard, Jessie. 1974. *The Future of Motherhood: Values and Options*. Chicago: Aldine Press.

Bernard, Jessie. 1979. "Policy and Women's Time." In Jean Lipman-Blumen and Jessie Bernard, eds., *Sex Roles and Social Policy*. Beverly Hills: Sage.

Bernard, Jessie. 1982. *The Future of Marriage*. 2d ed. New Haven: Yale University Press. (Originally published in 1972.)

Boon, James A. 1974. "Anthropology and Nannies." *Man* (March), pp. 137–40.

Bopp, Mary Louise. 1981. "Professional Women and Their Career Networks." Ed.D. dissertation, Teachers College, Columbia University.

Burke, W. Warner. 1982. "Leaders: Their Behavior and Development." In David A. Nadler, Michael Tushman, and Nina G. Hatvany, eds.,

Managing Organizations: Readings and Cases, pp. 237–45. Boston: Little, Brown.

Caplan, Paula J. and Ian Hall-McCorquodale. 1985. "Mother-Blaming in Major Clinical Journals." *American Journal of Orthopsychiatry* (July), 55(3):345–51.

Carlson, Bonnie E. (1982). "Preschoolers' Sex-Role Identity, Father-Role Perceptions, and Paternal Family Participation." In Joan Aldous, ed. *Two Paychecks: Life in Dual-Earner Families*, pp. 207–25. Beverly Hills: Sage.

Catalyst Career and Family Center. 1981. *Corporations and Two-Career Families: Directions for the Future*. New York: Catalyst.

Chess, Stella. 1982. "The 'Blame the Mother' Ideology." *International Journal of Mental Health* 11:95–107.

Chess, Stella and Alexander Thomas. 1982. "Infant Bonding: Mystique and Reality." *American Journal of Orthopsychiatry* (April), 52 (2):213–22.

Chess, Stella, Alexander Thomas, and Herbert G. Birch. 1965. *Your Child Is a Person*. New York: Penguin Books.

Columbia University Graduate School of Business, Office of Admission. 1982. Telephone interview.

Davis, Kingsley. 1984. "Wives and Work: The Sex Role Revolution and Its Consequences." *Population and Development Review* (September), 10(3):397–417.

Deutsch, Helene. 1944–45. *The Psychology of Women—A Psychoanalysis*. 2 vols. New York: Grune and Stratton.

Drummond, Lee. 1978. "The Transatlantic Nannies: Notes on a Comparative Semiotics of the Family in English-Speaking Societies." *American Ethnologist* 5:30–42.

Epstein, Cynthia Fuchs. 1970. *Woman's Place: Options and Limits in Professional Careers*. Berkeley: University of California Press.

Epstein, Cynthia Fuchs. 1981. *Women in Law*. New York: Basic Books.

Epstein, Cynthia Fuchs. 1983. "The New Total Woman." *Working Woman* (April), pp. 100–3.

Erikson, Erik. 1950. *Childhood and Society*. New York: W. W. Norton.

Erikson, Erik. 1968. *Identity, Youth, and Crisis*. New York: W. W. Norton.

Feinstein, Karen, ed. 1979. *Working Women and Families*. Beverly Hills: Sage.

Fogarty, Michael P., Rhona Rapoport, and Robert N. Rapoport. 1971. *Sex, Career, and Family*. London: Allen and Unwin.

Fowlkes, Martha. 1980. *Behind Every Successful Man*. New York: Columbia University Press.

Fraiberg, Selma. 1959. *The Magic Years*. New York: Scribner's.

Fraiberg, Selma. 1977. *Every Child's Birthright: In Defense of Mothering*. New York: Basic Books.

Friedan, Betty, 1963. *The Feminine Mystique*. New York: W. W. Norton.

Friedan, Betty. 1981. *The Second Stage*. New York: Summit Books.

Giele, Janet Zollinger. 1978. *Women and the Future: Changing Sex Roles in Modern America*. New York: Free Press.

Gilligan, Carol. 1982. *In a Different Voice: Psychological Theory and Women's Development*. Cambridge, Mass.: Harvard University Press.

Greenwald, Carol. 1980. *Highlights of the Literature: Women in Management*. Scarsdale, N.Y.: Work in America Institute.

Hennig, Margaret and Anne Jardim. 1976. *The Managerial Woman*. New York: Pocket Books, Simon and Schuster.

Hoffman, L. and F. I. Nye. 1974. "Effects on Children." In L. Hoffman and F. I. Nye, eds., *Working Mothers*. San Francisco: Jossey-Bass.

Horney, Karen. 1937. *The Neurotic Personality of Our Time*. London: Kegan Paul, Trench, Trubner.

Hunt, Janet G. and Larry L. Hunt. 1982a. "Dilemmas and Contradictions of Status: The Case of the Dual-Career Family." In Rachel Kahn-Hut, Arlene Kaplan Daniels, and Richard Colvard, eds., *Women and Work: Problems and Perspectives*, pp. 181–91. New York: Oxford University Press.

Hunt, Janet G. and Larry L. Hunt. 1982b. "Dual-Career Families: Vanguard of the Future or Residue of the Past?" In Joan Aldous, ed., *Two Paychecks: Life in Dual-Earner Families*, pp. 41–59. Beverly Hills: Sage.

Johnson, Colleen Leahy and Frank A. Johnson. 1980. "Parenthood, Marriage, and Careers: Situational Constraints and Role Strain." In Fran Pepitone-Rockwell, ed., *Dual-Career Couples*, pp. 143–61. Beverly Hills: Sage.

Kagan, Julia. 1983. "Survey: Work in the 1980s and 1990s." *Working Woman* (August), pp. 18, 20.

Kamerman, Sheila. 1980. *Parenting in an Unresponsive Society: Managing Work and Family Life*. New York: Free Press.

Kanter, Rosabeth Moss. 1977. *Men and Women of the Corporation*. New York: Basic Books.

Kanter, Rosabeth Moss. 1982. "The Impact of Hierarchical Structures on the Work Behavior of Women and Men." In Rachel Kahn-Hut, Arlene Kaplan Daniels, and Richard Colvard, eds., *Women and Work: Problems and Perspectives*, pp. 234–47. New York: Oxford University Press.

Kaplan, Louise J. 1978. *Oneness and Separateness: From Infant to Individual*. New York: Simon and Schuster.

Korn/Ferry International. 1982. *Profile of Women Senior Executives*. New York: Korn/Ferry International.

Kotter, John P. 1982. *The General Managers*. New York: Free Press.

Kundsin, Ruth B., ed. 1974. *Women and Success: The Anatomy of Achievement*. New York: William Morrow.

Larwood, Laurie and Marion M. Wood. 1977. *Women in Management*. Lexington, Mass.: Lexington Books, D. C. Heath.

Leichter, Hope Jensen, ed. 1977. *The Family as Educator*. New York: Teachers College Press.

Leichter, Hope Jensen. 1979. "Families and Communities as Educators: Some Concepts of Relationship." In Hope Jensen Leichter, ed., *Families and Communities as Educators*, pp. 3–94. New York: Teachers College Press.

Levinson, Daniel J. 1978. *The Seasons of a Man's Life.* New York: Alfred A. Knopf.

Lyons, Nona Plessner. 1983. "Two Perspectives: On Self, Relationships, and Morality." *Harvard Educational Review* (May), 53(2):125–45.

Malinowski, Bronislaw. 1922. *Argonauts of the Western Pacific.* London: Routledge.

Marks, Stephen R. 1977. "Multiple Roles and Role Strain: Some Notes on Human Energy, Time, and Commitment." *American Sociological Review* (December), 42:921–36.

Maslow, Abram. 1971. *The Farther Reaches of Human Nature.* New York: Viking Press.

Miller, Jean Baker, ed. 1973. *Psychoanalysis and Women.* Baltimore: Penguin Books.

Miller, Jean Baker. 1976. *Toward a New Psychology of Women.* Boston: Beacon Press.

Model, Suzanne. 1982. "Housework by Husbands: Determinants and Implications." In Joan Aldous, ed., *Two Paychecks: Life in Dual-Earner Families*, pp. 193–205. Beverly Hills: Sage.

Nadelson, Carol C. and Theodore Nadelson. 1980. "Dual-Career Families: Benefits and Costs." In Fran Pepitone-Rockwell, ed., *Dual-Career Couples*, pp. 91–109. Beverly Hills: Sage.

Neugarten, Dail Ann and Jay M. Shafritz, eds. 1980. *Sexuality in Organizations: Romantic and Coercive Behavior at Work.* Oak Park, Ill.: Moore.

Pepitone-Rockwell, Fran, ed. 1980. *Dual Career Couples.* Beverly Hills: Sage.

Peters, Thomas J. and Robert H. Waterman, Jr. 1982. *In Search of Excellence: Lessons from America's Best Run Companies.* New York: Warner Books.

Phelan, Gladys K., ed. 1979. *Family Relationships.* Minneapolis: Burgess.

Poloma Margaret M., Brian F. Pendleton, and T. Neal Garland. 1982. "Reconsidering the Dual-Career Marriage: A Longitudinal Approach." In Joan Aldous, ed., *Two Paychecks: Life in Dual-Earner Families*, pp. 173–92. Beverly Hills: Sage.

Poster, Mark. 1980. *Critical Theory of the Family.* New York: Seabury Press.

Rapoport, Rhona and Robert N. Rapoport. 1976. *Dual-Career Families Re-Examined.* New York: Harper and Row.

Rapoport, Rhona and Robert N. Rapoport. 1979. "Further Considerations on the Dual-Career Family." In Gladys K. Phelan, ed., *Family Relationships*, pp. 58–68. Minneapolis: Burgess.

Roland, Alan, and Barbara Harris, eds. 1979. *Sociohistorical and Psychoanalytical Perspectives on Career and Motherhood: Struggles for a New Identity.* New York: Human Science Press.

Rubin, Lillian. 1976. *Worlds of Pain*. New York: Basic Books.

St. John-Parsons, Donald. 1978. "Career and Family: A Study of Continuous Dual-Career Families." Ed. D. dissertation, Teachers College, Columbia University.

Shreve, Anita. 1984. "The Working Mother as Role Model." *New York Times Magazine*, September 9.

Sieber, Sam D. 1974. "Toward a Theory of Role Accumulation." *American Sociological Review* (August), 39:567–78.

Simpson, Ida Harper and Paula England. 1982. "Conjugal Work Roles and Marital Solidarity." In Joan Aldous, ed., *Two Paychecks: Life in Dual-Earner Families*, pp. 147–71. Beverly Hills: Sage.

Spradley, James P. 1979. *The Ethnographic Interview*. New York: Holt, Rinehart, and Winston.

Stack, Carol B. 1974. *All Our Kin*. New York: Harper and Row.

Tufte, Virginia and Barbara Myerhoff, eds. 1979. *Changing Images of the Family*. New Haven: Yale University Press.

U.S. Bureau of the Census. 1984. *Statistical Abstract of the United States: 1984*. Table 686. Washington, D.C.: Government Printing Office.

Varenne, Herve. 1977. *Americans Together: Structured Diversity in a Midwestern Town*. New York: Teachers College Press.

Warren, Mary Ann. 1982. "Is Androgyny the Answer to Sexual Stereotyping?" In Mary Vetterling-Braggin, ed., *"Femininity," "Masculinity," and "Androgyny,"* pp. 170–86. Totowa, N.J.: Littlefield, Adams.

Wessel, David. 1984. "Working Fathers Feel New Pressure Arising from Child-Rearing Duties." *Wall Street Journal*, September 7.

White, W. Robert. 1963. *Ego and Reality in Psychoanalytic Theory*. Psychological Issues, Monograph 2. New York: International Universities Press.

Yohalem, Alice M., ed. 1980. *Women Returning to Work: Policies and Progress in Five Countries*. Montclair, N.J.: Allanheld, Osmun.

Zimmerman, Irla Lee and Maurine Bernstein. 1983. "Parental Work Patterns in Alternate Families: Influence on Child Development." *American Journal of Orthopsychiatry* (July), 53(3):418–25.

Index